NO ACCESS
WASHINGTON, DC

NO ACCESS
WASHINGTON, DC

THE CAPITAL'S HIDDEN TREASURES, HAUNTS, AND FORGOTTEN PLACES

BETH KANTER

Photography by Emily Pearl Goodstein and Beth Kanter

Globe
Pequot

GUILFORD, CONNECTICUT

Globe
Pequot

An imprint of The Rowman & Littlefield Publishing Group, Inc.
4501 Forbes Blvd., Ste. 200
Lanham, MD 20706
www.rowman.com

Distributed by NATIONAL BOOK NETWORK

Photography by Emily Pearl Goodstein and Beth Kanter
Former Embassy of Iran interior photos on pages 38 and 39 are courtesy of Eric Parnes

British Library Cataloguing in Publication Information available
Library of Congress Cataloging-in-Publication Data available

ISBN 978-1-4930-3222-8 (paperback)
978-1-4930-3225-9 (e-book)

♾™ The paper used in this publication meets the minimum requirements of American National Standard for Information Sciences—Permanence of Paper for Printed Library Materials, ANSI/NISO Z39.48-1992

Printed in the United States of America

For Jeff

CONTENTS

INTRODUCTION

The sky shines blue above a spot where trash once smoldered. Stepping over the gravelly ground sprinkled with patches of grass working hard to grow, we head toward the stream. A slight downward slope, trees, and some brush conceal the water. The stream does not reveal its full self until our group of three stands practically at its edge.

It's picture perfect. (Convenient since we are there to take photos.) Camera ready with full trees in shades of late summer green that mask city life. Commuters, construction sites, tour buses, street vendors, traffic patterns, and national news live shots can neither be seen nor heard from where we stand. The very idea of them momentarily dissolves in the water. Its surface gleaming as it flows toward the nearby Anacostia River. While we take it all in, a sweet but slightly suspicious dog approaches. After inspecting us for a few minutes, she lets us scratch her ears. The friendly pup's owner, a man sitting on a green camping chair holding a fishing rod, also greets us. A yellow supermarket tray of boneless chicken breast, which he tells us makes for good bait, sits beside his tackle box. He's been baiting his hooks here on and off for years, mostly catching catfish and rockfish, but they haven't started biting yet today. Maybe they are too busy drinking in the view to feast on cubed chicken cutlets right now.

We chat for a while longer, petting the dog, marveling at the weather, as one does when presented with such a day. Photos are snapped, I scribble down notes and ask a few more questions. We need to get going, and it's time for us to stop scaring the fish away with our camera clicks, rustling paper, and footsteps. As we say our goodbyes, our fisherman friend points to the full trees across the stream. "Eagles build nests in those trees," he tells us. "They always come back to where they were born." Right then, as if on cue, a flock of eagles lifts out of the treetops. I cannot believe it. We cannot believe it. Our new friend just nods his head. He, of course, believes it. He knew it to be true all along.

It's a scene that keeps swirling around in my mind as I move through the process of putting together *No Access Washington, DC*. The notion of a secret shared through a place, be it by the riverside or inside a famous site, keeps coming back to me. There was nothing hidden about that site for the man who greeted us at the water in far Northeast that day. If anything, quite the opposite. But for us at that moment with those eagles and that exquisite blue sky, it felt like a secret shared or at least a shared truth.

I've been reminding myself often of that morning as I write *No Access Washington, DC*. I've been holding on to it throughout my journeying to what many don't, can't, or won't typically see here in town. It helps me remember that hidden is in the eye of the beholder. Access, too, of course.

This book is my riff on hidden DC and at times hidden DCs, plural. I approach it as a gift, a chance to show off the city I live in and love in a different way. The goal is to shine a light on all facets of the notion of hidden and all kinds of access—and to tell all kinds of stories through them. The result is the book you hold in your hands. It's a book that tells a story of Washington through places in, near, under, over, or around the city—a collection of spaces that most people don't see, can't see, rarely see, don't know how to see, or haven't seen. Each one tells a story, for *No Access Washington, DC* is at its core a place-forward narrative told through words and images that illuminate different kinds of hidden.

Sometimes we go beneath the city's most iconic building, as is the case of the massive undercroft below the Lincoln Memorial, complete with sweeping columns, vintage graffiti, and fully formed stalactites rarely seen by anyone other than the people charged with its care and security. At other times we shine a light on the hidden-in-plain-sight wonders of DC such as the forty boundary stones set down at the request of George Washington beginning in 1791 to create this city in the first place, the underfoot mini Washington Monument just a few feet away from the real thing that lurks beneath a locked utility hole, or the front lawn of a neighborhood home that for the past decade has been a thriving habitat for plastic dinosaurs that local kids pose and stage.

On some days we lay eyes on the Finnish embassy's invitation-only sauna society, the with-the-band VIP dressing room at the 9:30 Club, a sculptor's private studio, DC Brau's high-tech beer lab, or the members-only red dock with the white star at the Potomac Boat Club, arguably one of the most serene early-morning views in the city.

A handful of the places included in this book can only be viewed during a heartbeat in time, like the hundreds of acres of sunflowers that bloom for two weeks every summer in Poolesville, the last day at a historic downtown auction house, or the annual children's Halloween naturalization ceremony in a Fairfax immigration office.

Still others on these pages are concealed above or below the city's most visited and most recognizable landmarks, like the archives of the National Building Museum, the bell tower high in the National Cathedral, or the crypt below it where Helen Keller and Annie Sullivan are interred. At times it's about a place that protects thousands of previously privately held memories, like the emotionally charged National Park Service's Museum Resource Center, where curators carefully catalog and preserve everything that has been left at the Vietnam Veterans Memorial.

No Access Washington, DC is an armchair tour of all these places and many more. Through the photographs and the words collected here, my hope is for you to share in the experience of them. In many ways, this book is a love letter to DC, a tribute to a side not shown on postcards but gaze-worthy all the same.

Through the exercise of curating *No Access Washington, DC*, I've also attempted to go beyond the flat DC of the political cartoons and stump speeches to spend time in the multidimensional city almost 700,000 real people call home. More often than not it is the people who live here who carry on, build, preserve, study, and care for the places visitors, tourists, and politicians interact with within our town. While place is the protagonist on these pages, there always are people in the background or foreground. You may have to squint to see them, but they are there. They are the invisible threads connecting the stories on these pages to each other and connecting us to them. They know where the stories are kept and generously tell them without demanding the final word. They remind us of what is good and what is complicated and what is both. They know where to look for the eagles and remind us of our instinct to come back home.

AVALON THEATRE

For the price of a ticket, the Avalon Theatre transports movie-goers everywhere in the world—and occasionally beyond—five shows a day, seven days a week. But what most who belly up to the box office don't know is that there is an unscripted journey to be had behind the silver screen at the 1923 Chevy Chase movie house.

For the lucky few who get to see it, the area concealed by the screen serves as a faded, largely untouched snapshot of the historic theater's early days. It reveals chipped, dusty clues about a time when the names of live acts graced the marquee, an organ played during silent films, and some 1,200 people (versus the 450 seats there now) squeezed together to take it all in. Decrepit dressing rooms where actors once made quick costume changes still stand in the wings, and peeling gold paint adorns what appears to be a once-gilded arch above the stage now partly concealed by wooden pallets, plywood, and the stray piece of aging movie equipment. Beneath the stage, a large pit, once an important part of a cooling system, remains.

"They got AC in the thirties," explains former board chair Kim Abraham. "Before that they had a system where they would dump ice and circulate the air one way or another around it. It was a comfortable place to come and get out of the heat. People would settle in here for the day."

Abraham joined with others in the community to save the Avalon when it was abruptly closed in 2001. As a result of their efforts, the theater reopened in 2003 as an independent, nonprofit entity. Money raised during the process allowed the Avalon to be repaired and reimagined as a film and education center.

"The previous owner had plans to gut it and turn it into a two-story retail thing," says Executive Director Bill Oberdorfer, another of the original community member group who joined together to save the theater. "The façade was somewhat protected. It's landmarked. But the rest . . . The standing joke here is that the only reason this is not a CVS is that there is one down the street."

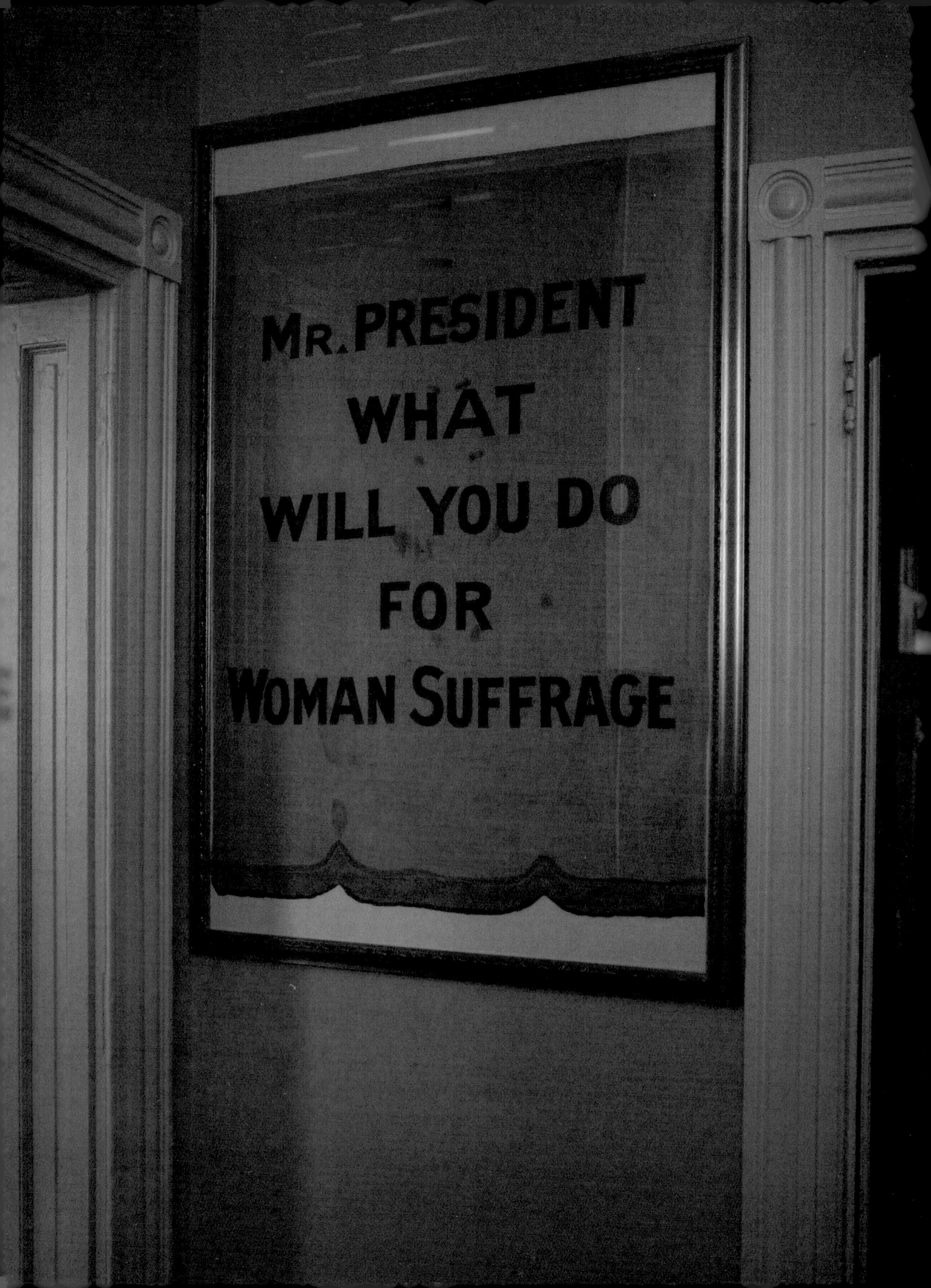
MR. PRESIDENT
WHAT
WILL YOU DO
FOR
WOMAN SUFFRAGE

BELMONT-PAUL WOMEN'S EQUALITY NATIONAL MONUMENT AND THE FLORENCE BAYARD HILLES FEMINIST LIBRARY

The four hundred or so notecards found in the collection of the Florence Bayard Hilles Feminist Library at the Belmont-Paul Women's Equality National Monument are worth far more than the yellowed paper they are written on. Although ordinary looking, the cards make up what in 1915 was a cutting-edge system that helped secure the vote for women in this country.

"Besides being the first people to picket the White House, the suffragists also really innovated and changed the way people lobby," says Jana Friesen McCabe, a supervisory park ranger with the monument. "Their strategy was to bring in women from all over the country to lobby, which was not done before. If you are doing that, how do you prevent [the members] from getting the same story over and over again? How do you keep track of the progress? By taking detailed notes . . . incredibly detailed notes on where Congress stood, whether they were married, if their wife supported the amendment, if their daughter did."

The National Women's Party Congressional Voting Cards kept track of the good, the bad, and the ugly. "So vehemently opposed," reads one card documenting a congressional visit. "Almost insulting in his insinuations in that we are not normal women because we do not want to be protected as we should. 'The normal woman knows her place,' he says. There is no hope for him, I am sure. And he should be avoided as far as possible. He opposes the amendment on the grounds that [it was a state's right to decide who should be able to vote] and also on the principles of everlasting inferiority of women."

Harsh words like these were slung not only at the women lobbying Congress but also at their system. "Word got out somehow that they were doing this, and people started to refer to it as the 'deadly political index,'" tells the National Women's Party's Director of Interpretation Kelsey Millay. "They saw it as weird and intrusive that they were keeping such thorough records on people."

While a commonplace approach today, the Congressional Voting Cards set a lobbying precedent. The "deadly index" in part grew out of what was considered one of the only acceptable jobs for a woman in the early part of the twentieth century. "At the time, one of the few professions opened to them was to be a secretary," says McCabe. "They took those skills and applied them to this fight for suffrage."

Historical treasures like the cards share space with the other significant artifacts and collections preserved at Florence Bayard Hilles Feminist Library, the country's first of its kind. The actual poles the activists used to hold up their banners in front of the White House lean against a wall near the library's entrance. A small sampling of them also decorates the walls of the staircase in the public part of the Capitol Hill house that served as the National Women's Party headquarters from 1929 to 1997. In 1997 it transformed from a lobbying group to a nonprofit educational organization. A collection of scrapbooks detailing the party's life remains a library highlight.

"The house is named for Alva Belmont, who is the wealthy benefactor of the women's movement, and Alice Paul, who was the founder," Millay explains. "Alva Belmont collected newspaper clippings about suffrage and about the National Women's Party. Being a very wealthy woman, she then would hire people to create scrapbooks."

Some of the banners raised on those poles can be seen in action in the newspaper photos preserved among the pages of these meticulously kept scrapbooks that span decades. A select few are on display in the public part of the house.

In 2016 the historic site officially became part of the National Park Service. History truly pours out of every corner of this site. Take the attic space now used as an office for the rangers: The vintage floral wallpaper in the bathroom harkens back to the time when women boarded in the house. Since unmarried women were not allowed to check into hotels, many of the activists also lived or stayed in the house through the years even as recently as the early 1990s.

Maryland,

Harrington, Emerson C.
Democrat

(home address) Cambridge, Md.
(other) ....

The Suffragist

(The National Women's Party now operates out of the red brick home's basement.) Its mission now is to move the house and movement's lore from the lesser-known history to the more broadly shared category through the park service and its interpreters.

"It's such an incredible story, and it's one that doesn't get told often or widely enough," McCabe shares. "I consider myself well educated. I took women's studies classes. I took history classes. I knew about the connection between suffrage and abolitionism. I read the second-wave feminist philosophers, but there was nothing in retrospect on this period. There were no classes offered. I had never heard about Alice Paul before. I never even questioned how the Nineteenth Amendment got passed. When I first heard about it, I almost felt like I had been cheated.

"These were incredible women. They were so dedicated. They went through so much to secure the right to vote for us, and yet they are left out of curriculum, even curriculum that celebrates women. To get to be part of sharing that story and hopefully raising the visibility of it . . . is something I never dreamed I would get to do in my career, let alone to get to do something that is so personally meaningful to me."

BOUNDARY STONES OF THE DISTRICT OF COLUMBIA

One is in a church parking lot, another lies within eyeshot of a fast-food restaurant, two blend into the background at old cemeteries, while several others hang out at the edge of parking lots or pop up in people's backyards. Hidden in and out of plain sight, the forty boundary stones set down in 1791 and 1792 to define the young nation's new capital city are considered the country's first monuments, notwithstanding the lack of fanfare surrounding them.

A cross between worn grave markers and crude replicas of the Washington Monument, the sandstone boundaries form a ten-mile square—a 3D connect-the-dot map of the original District of Columbia, with one stone placed every mile along the periphery. Many of the surveying markers haven't aged gracefully. Largely unprotected and often forgotten, the stones have been the victims of weather, construction, and, in at least one case, a bulldozer. Four no longer exist and have been replaced with replicas.

Two of the most pristine examples of what the stones—and the area—looked like when Major Andrew Ellicott placed them in the ground at President George Washington's request hide on the grounds of the Washington Aqueduct. They carry the numbers NW4 and NW5.

"Probably my favorite is NW5 because it's the most pristine," says Stephen Powers, cochair of the Nation's Capital Boundary Stones Committee. "It's among those in the

stone enthusiast. "I kept journals with drawings and maps documenting what I saw."

The stones first captured his curiosity when he was helping his then elementary school–age daughter with a homework project. Taken by the history and provenance of the simple monuments from George Washington's day, he now works to bring attention and, he hopes, protection to them year-round.

"Everything in the area is a result of these stones," Powers says. "The Beltway goes around a ten-mile square because of the way the DC lines were drawn. Look at a map of the DMV, and the most prominent thing is that ten-mile square. It's all because of that line. It's because of the fact that these stones sat in the ground untouched for [so many] years while everything grew around them. They tell the story of [almost 230] years of history and growth."

Other than the occasional downed tree, little has changed around the two stones on the campus of the water treatment plant. During Powers's early visits to NW4 and NW5, a now-retired longtime plant employee would describe how members of the Daughters of the American Revolution made annual pilgrimages to the spot.

"He told lots of stories about how the DAR used to come out yearly and have

best condition of the forty since fewer people have been able to get there because it's in the middle of the woods [and on private property]. It really gives you a feel for the terrain Ellicott had to traverse."

For the past almost fifteen years, on the first Sunday in May, Powers sets out early to visit all forty stones by nightfall. He records what has changed around them and which ones might need repair or a crew of volunteers to pick up trash cluttering them. "When I started, there was no digital photography or Internet," says the boundary picnics in front of the stones," Powers recalls. "They were all in dresses and sashes, and he would set up picnic tables for them. They would come to praise the stones."

All of the stones carry the inscription "Jurisdiction of the United States" on the side facing the District. The opposite sides say either "Virginia" or "Maryland," depending on which state ceded the land to create the city.

Small cage-like fences put up by local chapters of the Daughters of the American Revolution in the early 1900s enclose some of the stones currently found in DC, Maryland, and Virginia, reflecting the fact that the city no longer is a perfect ten-mile square. The very first fence sponsored was for the water plant stones.

The Washington Aqueduct general manager, Thomas Jacobus, reports that he gets calls about once a month from people wanting to view NW4 and NW5. He honors those requests when possible, sometimes driving groups in a company van and then leading the way to the stones through overgrowth and forest with a walking stick in hand.

As more people find out about the boundary stones, interest in them seems to increase. Northern Virginia resident Craig Fifer counts himself among the fan club of the city markers. After reading about them on Facebook, he decided to set the goal of seeing all forty the year before he turned forty. "Perhaps it's the balance between the enjoyment of finding new things and the satisfaction of a finite accomplishment," Fifer says of the draw to the stones that were placed in the ground at a time when both the White House and Capitol still were under construction. "In terms of NW4 and NW5, I think they're a reminder not only that we have so many treasures hidden in plain sight in our region but that you can see most of them up close if you just ask nicely."

CAPITOL STONES IN ROCK CREEK PARK

Piles of discarded pieces from the Capitol have been gathering moss off-trail in Rock Creek Park for decades. Weathered by time, the stones that were once part of the façade of the US Capitol have taken on the green hue of the quiet forest around them. Yet the architectural remnants still manage to marvel when viewed for the first time in this unlikely spot. Elegantly carved corner pieces and decorative motifs grace some of the larger pieces that sit among large slabs stacked in uneven piles. Many of them have numbers etched on the sides, which speak to a more ordered time, while graffiti on a few comes courtesy of years of neglect.

The origin story of the sandstones in the park goes back to 1958, when Congress decided to expand the east façade of the US Capitol and rebuild it in marble. Switching from sandstone to marble was controversial, according to newspaper reports from the time. The marble camp won, and workers carefully removed and catalogued the sandstones. However, a clear plan for what to do with the hundreds of pieces taken from the building did not exist. At first they were kept on the grounds of the Capitol Power Plant. Around 1975 they were moved to the current location—off the beaten path in Rock Creek Park not far from the Rock Creek Park Horse Center, where they remain.

CARTER G. WOODSON HOME
NATIONAL HISTORIC SITE

Kerry Wilson points toward an empty room near the rear of the historic Shaw townhouse. "The kitchen was back here," says the park ranger, her voice bouncing off the blank walls and the newly restored original hardwood floors. "There is a story of Dr. Woodson walking into the kitchen and one of the students who lived here was scrubbing the floor. Dr. Woodson said to this student, 'I don't pay you to wash the floor. I need you to go write and do your research and produce.' Then he took over cleaning the floors himself."

The interaction says volumes about Dr. Carter G. Woodson, the man known as the father of African American history, and the significant role his home played in furthering his work. The first African American man of enslaved parents to earn a PhD from Harvard University, Dr. Woodson lived on the third floor of 1538 Ninth Street, NW, from 1922 until 1950, when he died. The educator and scholar wrote, studied, and mentored students here, many of whom, like the young man he discovered cleaning the kitchen, also resided here. From the first floor, Dr. Woodson ran the organization now known as the Association for the Study of African American Life and History, or ASALH, which he founded in 1915. Within these walls, he created Negro History Week, which went on to become Black History Month. Out of this once-bustling house, Dr. Woodson also ran a publishing company called the Associated Publishers, Inc., which gave a platform for a range of important African American voices during a time when they could not have been published elsewhere. Scholarly journals on the African American story that countered racist theories were composed and edited within these walls as were numerous papers on almost every aspect of Black life in America. Remarkably, Dr. Woodson, who worked in a coal mine until he was twenty, accomplished all of this during the Jim Crow era, when DC was still a segregated town. The list of accomplishments that rose from this address goes on and on.

Following Dr. Woodson's death, his once-vibrant home suffered neglect. But after years of careful restoration, his townhouse, a National Historic Site now part of the National Park Service, opened to the public in 2017.

"This building fell into serious disrepair," Wilson says of the home. "We essentially had to rebuild it. It took about ten years to bring the property to a place where it could be opened. We have very little of his original furniture. And different schools [such as Howard University, where he once served as a dean] now have a lot of his original books

and writings. But all of those bricks in front were here when Carter G. was here, so he probably touched them or leaned against them."

Exhibit creation and interpretation are the next two phases for the historic site, which include a bookstore and an office for ASALH. It already gives visitors a glimpse of what the house and neighborhood felt like when Dr. Woodson and his students resided here.

"It wasn't all office buildings then," Wilson says. "It was pretty vibrant here. There were lots of bars around. The church right next door is the one that he would go to. The YMCA is right across the street. He would actually go have lunch with the ladies over there. He was a working part of the neighborhood."

Future plans for the Carter G. Woodson Home National Historic Site will shine light on the different aspects of his life and work, including plans for joint programming with the nearby Mary McLeod Bethune Council House National Historic Site. (Bethune and Woodson were contemporaries, colleagues, and friends.) Until then, something about the empty rooms feels profound. It also means almost no part of the house is off limits to visitors yet, an unusual situation for a historic home. The freedom to experience the house as a sort of blank slate while

meditating the depth of what was done here often does not happen at more established historic sites.

"His study was here and his bedroom was in there," Wilson says, and continues the tour of the empty house. "I like to think of the windows being opened and a summer breeze coming in and the music and noise of the city he heard."

DC BRAU

Safety glasses are required on the DC Brau production floor. Beer goggles, they're optional. A few feet away in the high-tech beer lab, eyewear is dealer's choice as long as the focus stays laser sharp on the science of the brew.

"In this lab we actually do two types of analysis now," says then lab manager Juan Moreno while standing in the Brau lab, which looks like a small, well-funded medical laboratory fit inside a generously sized galley kitchen. "[At first] we were only doing microbiological analysis. Seeing what types of things are growing in the beer that shouldn't be there. Or, better, finding out that indeed nothing is growing. Now we've also moved on to analytical analysis, which actually gives us numbers and figures that we can attach to color, flavors, off flavors, and bitterness, too."

A home-brewer-turned-professional-brewer, Moreno demonstrates the equipment in his analysis bag of tricks. Some are readily recognizable from high school biology, such as the centrifuge that spins down samples or the microscope for counting yeast cells. Others carry names and purposes specific to the beer industry . . . or a really crazy fantasy high school science class. The lab's newest acquisition could star in either scenario. "It's actually looking for the DNA itself," he says of the machine. "It's kind of cutting edge and has recently been introduced to the brewing industry. We jumped on the chance to have it."

Yes, beer DNA.

"We bought it for our expansion so we can benchmark our current products," Moreno continues. "With new equipment come different flavor profiles. Before, we

would sit down at a round table and do sensory and say, yeah, this tastes like porter even though one of us just had coffee."

Moreno estimates that he spends roughly 60 percent of his time in the Brau lab. The rest of his time is spent on the floor, specifically the tunnel lined with a white board displaying much of the same information shown on the screen of the lab computer that runs special brew software. Unlike the quiet of the laboratory, on the floor, music blares over the buzz of the equipment, pallets of empty cans rumble by, and a Kelly Towles painted tank named Solomon G. Grundy smiles at the staff. The "G" stands for Guardian, and unlike his poetic namesake and more like the comic book character, he's stuck around for more than week. A "superfriend of the Brau," Grundy gazes ahead with drunken eyes, apparently the only DC Brau rep allowed to don beer goggles while on the clock.

DINOSAUR HOUSE

Barbara and David Turnham's front yard proves that a grandparent's love will never become extinct. When the couple's now-preteen grandson was about two years old, they placed a collection of toy dinosaurs in front of their North Cleveland Park house for him. The assortment of plastic prehistoric creatures of different shapes, colors, and sizes wound up delighting their grandson as well the neighborhood kids. When he lost interest in the creatures a couple of years later, the Turnhams gathered up the Jurassic still life and brought it inside. The local kids did not approve of the landscaping change.

"Immediately we got feedback—or push back—from parents and babysitters wanting to know what had happened and seeking restoration of the status quo," David shares. "We were happy to oblige and have continued the tradition ever since."

The yard is perfect for the whimsical display. The Turnhams' house, which they have lived in since 1972, sits on an incline with the several dozen mismatched dinosaurs striking poses on the part closest to the street. Rocks, pebbles, and greenery create the backdrop for the dinosaurscape along with a brick retaining wall that separates the property from the sidewalk and just happens to stand at toddler eye level. Little hands like to make scenes with the figurines, often placing the small dinosaurs in the

mouths of the larger ones and even creating classroom scenes with the animals.

"We very much enjoy—and who does not—watching toddlers and early speakers clambering over the rocks clutching their favorites," he shares. "Also, the adults inculcating lessons about property rights . . . at the end of the visit. Of course, we do lose one or two but also receive additions, so the dino population more or less balances out."

Several years ago that balance was completely thrown off. Every last one of the toys was stolen in the middle of the night. "We put out a notice explaining what had happened in the faint and unrealized hope that a guilty conscience would lead to restitution," Turnham recalls. "Instead we received a vast outpouring of new stock, including packages from Amazon and others accompanied by notes, some composed and written by the children themselves who donated one of their toys. This episode reinforced the feeling that we are now the humble custodians of a neighborly tradition."

DUPONT
UNDERGROUND

DUPONT UNDERGROUND

Art can grow anywhere. Even sandwiched between a perpetually congested traffic circle and the Red Line.

Dupont Underground planted its urban arts and culture venue in that exact location with the belief that an area below the surface could make for fertile ground. The curious spot for a nonprofit arts organization originally was part of a 75,000-square-foot tunnel network and trolley station. In 1949 the city moved the streetcars underground when they approached Dupont Circle to relieve traffic when more and more Americans embraced car ownership for the first time and more and more cities like DC started contending with traffic for the first time.

Trollies drove in and out of the station through two entrances—one at Connecticut Avenue and N Street and the other at Connecticut and R Street. After reemerging on the avenue, the trolleys continued along the regular street-level routes. Closed and covered by trees long ago, both openings were not far from the current Connecticut Avenue tunnel that let drivers bypass the circle. Pedestrian stairways to the platforms peppered the circle's perimeter.

A little more than ten years after the station opened, the city's streetcar system shut down permanently, and the station was abandoned. Save for a brief stint as a designated fallout shelter during the Cold War and later, in the 1990s, as a food court gone very wrong, the space sat empty, sealed off, and largely forgotten. An architect and the founder of Dupont Underground stumbled upon one of the closed pedestrian entrances. From there an idea was born, a lease with the city for the east side of the area was secured, and art was imagined. Then a lot of work needed to happen.

"It was pretty much a mess," says Chief Executive Officer Susan Corrigan. "What was here was all piled up. There was lots of junk."

Following the cleanup and prep effort, the challenge of running an art site with no lighting needed addressing. "What we have here that's different from any other art space is that we don't have any light," Corrigan explains. "So we use that. We use that by [bringing in] any kind of art that you generally would be able to see in the darkness, like film. The art brings the light."

Projectors flash huge images of contemporary pieces on the wall, art created to be ingested in just this way. Sound or music often accompanies the art. Visitors walk the curve of the former tracks right alongside the installations. "You feel small next to those big pieces of art," Corrigan says. "You are looking at it in a way you probably couldn't in art galleries and museums. And that's purposeful, too."

Dupont Underground also hosts film festivals, book readings, concerts, performance art, lectures, and other programs all with a distinct point of view and modern bent chosen to harmonize with the setting. Bright graffiti art, commissioned by some of the District's most well known graffiti artists, fills the walls opposite the projected images and sometimes seems to glow in its wake.

"This motion softens the hard edge of the graffiti," she observes. "It works together. You can see the beauty we have created here."

SAUNA DIPLOMA

Mr. John Smith
is hereby officially certified to be a member of the

Diplomatic Finnish Sauna Society

and an Honorary Spokesperson for Finnish Sauna Culture

The Diplomatic Finnish Sauna Society of D.C. is governed by the Embassy of Finland's Media Office. A person who has taken the sauna challenge and endured the 180° F heat is invited to join the Society and granted the title of "Honorary Spokesperson for Finnish Sauna Culture". The core idea of the Society is to exchange breaking D.C. news and hot scoops, create buzz and get refreshed in good company. The task of the Society is to spread the word about the joys of Finnish sauna culture and other great achievements of Finns inside and outside the Capitol Beltway.

June 7, 2017, Washington, D.C.

Sanna Kangasharju
Press Counselor
Embassy of Finland to the United States

Suomi
Finland
100

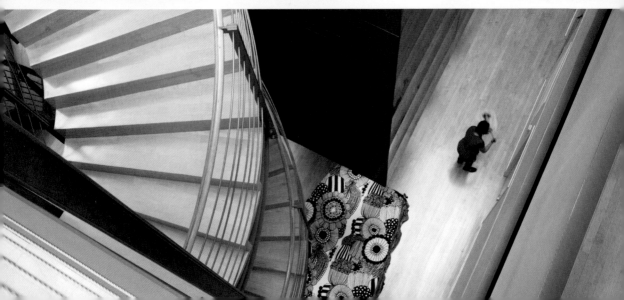

EMBASSY OF FINLAND, WASHINGTON, DC, AND THE DIPLOMATIC SAUNA SOCIETY

It's the hottest ticket in town. Walking into that joke is easy. Almost too easy. Stepping into the Embassy of the Republic of Finland's sauna, on the other hand, is a maneuver that requires some doing.

Once a month, the embassy opens its ground-level sauna to a handpicked few. With its hard-to-score invite, signature cocktail, and Who's Who of a guest list, the Diplomatic Sauna Society sounds like many other inside-the-beltway events save for one difference: the dress code. At this party, guests spend about half the night wrapped in big, fluffy towels.

"It's not that we invented something sort of superficial to be something different," says the Finnish embassy's press counselor, Sanna Kangasharju, who runs the society. "The embassy has a sauna, and we love that the local people get a chance to experience it."

Most Finns first experience a sauna as toddlers, and the typical Finnish family uses one at least once a week. Apartment buildings that do not have saunas in the individual flats offer communal ones, and each unit gets assigned a specific time to take advantage of it. In Finland, almost all special occasions, even Christmas dinner, are preceded by a sauna. At one time, Finnish women would even give birth in the sauna. "The sauna is such a huge part of our culture," Kangasharju shares.

The act of going to the sauna is so connected to the country's identity that every Finnish embassy in the world has a sauna, not just the DC location. "It's extremely relaxing, especially in the summertime, if you go for a swim in the lake or the ocean first," says Emilia Honkasaari, the embassy's communications coordinator. "You feel very much alive and clean afterward. If you have been there with your friends, you wind up having great discussions."

The Washington embassy's Diplomatic Sauna Society carries the Finnish sauna experience to town. Non-Finnish guests seem to have had an easy time embracing the tradition, seeing it as a way to unwind after a long week. The gatherings often last past midnight. The fact that guests cannot take their cell phones in the sauna and that the adjoining gray-and-white lounge and bar area offers spotty reception enhances the unwinding portion of the program.

"Normally, when I have a sauna society, we will have between twenty and twenty-five people," says Kangasharju, who issues branded society diplomas and T-shirts to all participants. "We don't do co-ed. I always go first with the ladies, and my husband goes with the men. When the ladies are in the sauna, the men are eating at the buffet dinner. Once the ladies are done, the men go in. We have a sauna bar going all night long."

Kangasharju carefully guards the identities of society members but does admit to hosting her fair share of "well-known names" since she took over the club from her predecessor in 2012. "We have a kind of rule: What happens in the sauna stays in the sauna," she says with a smile. "We have had famous journalists and musicians. But it varies a lot. Sometimes we have Washington reporters or Hill staff. We have had what we call a bank sauna for people from the World Bank."

Beyond the soothing heat of the sauna and its pretty lounge, the rest of the embassy similarly is steeped in Finnish style and sensibility with a dash of American influence thrown in for good measure. Perhaps this is best experienced when standing at the base of its stairway—a modern interpretation of an old Hollywood spiral staircase that leads to an open entertaining space on the main level.

"When you stand between the copper box and the wall, you feel like you are at the bottom of a canyon," Honkasaari states. "The architects [came up with] this idea when they were driving around the United States right before they finalized the drawings. They went to the Grand Canyon, and they were so impressed that they wanted to recreate the feeling. So even though the building has a very Finnish feeling when you step inside, it also has American features."

From this vantage point guests can drink in the surprising forest-like view through the back of the greening copper building. A long,

peaceful, glass-enclosed walkway peppered with Marimekko lounge pillows appears to hang among the trees. "When you approach the building from Massachusetts Avenue, it looks like it's one level; but then once you are inside the building, you see that you are actually on a pretty steep hill," Honkasaari explains while standing on the walkway between the indoor and outdoor space.

Along with the green view and façade, the Finnish embassy also embraces a green outlook. The environmentally conscious building stands out as one of the most efficient in town. Daylight is employed whenever possible to light offices and public space; efficient heating and air-conditioning systems are regulated closely; all offices have windows that can be opened; plants grow on the building's façade, providing a layer of shade from the DC sun; and finger foods are served at receptions, eliminating the need for plastic utensils.

The deliberate intent behind everything from the architectural plans of the embassy to its sauna society shines through with the natural light that bathes it, creating a soothing and welcoming space for those fortunate enough to pass through it.

"It's a very peaceful workplace," Honkasaari says.

FORMER EMBASSY OF IRAN, WASHINGTON, DC

Unbeknownst to most of the commuters who pass it on Massachusetts Avenue, almost no one has been inside the once-grand embassy that was abruptly sealed off and stands frozen in time.

A tomb. That's how photographer Eric Parnes describes the former Iranian embassy. He is one of the few people who has ventured inside since it was shuttered in 1979 during the Iran hostage crisis.

"Usually, things are not sealed off like this," says Parnes, an American Iranian artist who spent about an hour photographing the former embassy in 2013. "They either are demolished or repurposed."

For almost four decades, 3005 Massachusetts Avenue, NW, has sat locked and empty. Although the United States and Iran ended diplomatic relations in 1980, the Vienna Convention on Diplomatic Relations legally requires the United States to protect diplomatic properties when countries sever relations. The State Department fulfills this obligation by maintaining the property, as well as the former ambassador's residence next door, making sure the grass is cut, the snow removed, and other general exterior upkeep and security maintained. As Parnes's striking photos on pages 38 and 39 illustrate, the inside remains untouched. Parnes, who grew up in the area, will not disclose how he gained access to the interior of the former embassy located on a busy stretch of Embassy Row.

"I was swept with varied emotions from excitement to fear to sorrow," he says of his time inside the building.

During the 1960s and 1970s, legendary parties were held here with the champagne, caviar, and other indulgences provided without end. Andy Warhol, Barbra Streisand, Henry Kissinger, Elizabeth Taylor, Kirk Douglas, Gregory Peck, Mikhail Baryshnikov, and Liza Minnelli were among those who made the guest lists in the prerevolution heyday. Movie stars, heads of state, and royalty mingled beneath the high mirror-tiled ceiling in the dreamlike "Persian Room."

"The embassy is extremely large, but when devoid of people, its size imbues a sense of melancholy and emotional emptiness," Parnes reflects. "It would be fair to say that the historical remnants within the embassy figuratively haunt me. I used my camera as a method to contextualize the experience and question what that moment in time when the embassy closed both ended and created."

Born a few months after the revolution, Parnes remembers his family, friends, and now others after seeing his photo recounting stories about the embassy and its striking interior. "Stories [I've been told] included a man recalling his first kiss when he took a blanket with a young woman outside of the embassy to sit on the adjacent lawn of the Iranian ambassador's [house] to a woman's incredibly detailed account of the elegant food served and presented at an event to honor her father and his colleagues," he shares. "What [often] triggered these memories was [driving by] the embassy on Massachusetts Avenue. It is interesting because the embassy is very noticeable and well situated via its location, yet for most people its very existence is unknown and/or a mystery and appears forcefully hidden."

The gold in the mosaic design on the building's facade still shines in the sunlight as commuters drive past it every day. Only upon closer examination can the cracks, weathering, and worn patches be noticed on the structure that marries midcentury and Persian aesthetics. Through the side windows, slivers of the elaborate floral mosaics created by famous Iranian artists can be seen from the right viewpoint. The same holds true for what remains of an interior courtyard.

"Perhaps," Parnes shares, "what is most remarkable is that so much of the character of the space is still able to communicate to us even as it slowly falls apart."

FREDERICK DOUGLASS NATIONAL HISTORIC SITE

While the old house atop Cedar Hill tells the story of Frederick Douglass, the small house behind it holds the story of those who watch over it. Nested in the shadow of the historic home, the two-room Caretaker's Cottage did not exist in Douglass's day, but it did and does play an important part in the preservation of the property and the Frederick Douglass narrative.

In 1928, the National Association of Colored Women (NACW) built the simple home to help preserve the abolitionist's estate and legacy. The Frederick Douglass Memorial and Historical Association hired the individuals who worked and lived there until the National Park Service took over the property in the mid-1960s. Gladys Parham, the estate's final caretaker, resided in the cottage for more than thirty years, beginning in 1949. In 1965 the National Park Service hired her, and she lived there until her death in 1983.

"In 1949, the Frederick Douglass Memorial Historical Association appointed Mrs. Parham a caretaker of the Douglass home," reads Parham's *Washington Post* obituary. "For the next 16 years, she conducted tours of the home, cleaned the house and kept the lawns as a volunteer. In 1965, she was hired by the National Park Service to continue this work and did so until her death."

Today the renovated cottage acts as the ranger station for the Frederick Douglass National Historic Site. Parham's former living room is now an office devoted, as she was, to sharing with the public "everything Douglass" from his Anacostia estate.

GARUDA AVIARY LIFE LONG SANCTUARY FOR PARROTS AND THE KUNZANG PALYUL CHÖLING TEMPLE

High-pitched squeaks, shrill squawks, and unnerving shrieks rise up from a small corner of the rural Maryland campus that houses a Buddhist temple and monastery. The unmelodic and far from meditative sounds grow louder as one approaches its brightly colored source: dozens of rescue parrots who live on the temple grounds.

The Garuda Aviary, a lifelong sanctuary for parrots, takes in neglected, abused, and abandoned birds that have been given up by owners who realize the ills associated with domesticating parrots. The "We Bite" sign on the outdoor enclosure where the birds have "supervised playtime" shines light on one of the issues. The other challenges run deeper.

"Parrots that are bred in domestic settings are almost guaranteed to pull out their feathers," explains Christopher Zeoli, who runs Garuda Aviary along with a team of volunteers. Many of the volunteers, like Zeoli, are associated with the Kunzang Palyul Chöling Buddhist Temple. "It's an anxiety disorder. It's like trichotillomania."

When the birds pull out their feathers, it leads to blood loss, nerve damage, and other health problems that can result in the death of the animal. Parrot mills have contributed to the number of birds with these problems, according to Zeoli, who has devoted his life to the cause. Many of the birds under his care have raw, plucked bellies and wings. Some wear special vests or shirts he makes to help protect them from nipping at particularly vulnerable spots.

"In the wild, the birds would be preening their feathers with their beaks to keep their feathers clean, and that is a reassuring habit," Zeoli explains. "In a domestic setting, where they have too much anxiety and not enough to do with it, they preen too much, too hard, and too often. At some point they will pull out a feather that wasn't ready to go. They get a little bit of pain that goes with that, and it supplies them with a kind of endorphin. The birds think maybe now they know how to control their anxiety, and then they start pulling out their feathers in large amounts."

Most of the Garuda Aviary parrots suffer from the plucking disorder, a condition that does not go away. "It's basically impossible to help them stop," Zeoli states. "They need, in the first couple of years of their life, to be with their own kind, being taught how not to do those things. The birds that don't see their parents are almost guaranteed to go plucking out their feathers. The ones bred by people are missing fundamental self-nurturing skills."

Zeoli started taking care of unwanted parrots at eighteen, when his mother, one of the temple's founders, took up the cause, and they created a makeshift sanctuary in their garage in Arizona. The pair eventually brought the birds to Poolesville and started Garuda Aviary. Many of those birds remain part of the Maryland flock, which has increased with time and now includes more than fifty African grey parrots and cockatoos. Zeoli says he gets between one and three calls a week from people wanting to give up their birds.

Garuda Aviary's indoor area is filled with cages and has three distinct areas for different species. An enclosed breezeway attaches it to the enclosed outdoor space where birds are taken to play together when the temperature outside reaches at least 65 degrees. The public may visit the parrots when they are outside.

Once Zeoli and his team take in a bird, they commit to keeping it for life. They do not put up for adoption any of the animals that come under their care. Since parrots can live almost as long as humans, this is a long-term commitment. At almost fifty years old, a bird named Harry currently ranks as the flock's oldest member. Harry suffered abuse before being rescued and was terrified of humans for many years. "When I first met him just a few years into this whole thing [with my mom], if a human was in the room, he was freaking out," Zeoli says. "Now you look at him, and he is just as engaged and calm as the birds that are used to people. It's been a long rehabilitation."

THE HAY-ADAMS

A worn regal finish accentuates the decorative detailing adorning the ceiling of the Off the Record bar. The same golden stain delicately covers the fireplace mantel and the moldings of the bar located in the basement of the historic Hay-Adams hotel.

Or so it seems.

"It's cigar smoke not gold etching," explains Ashley Wood of the hotel's sales and marketing team. Yet again demonstrating that not everything in this town is how it first appears. "We can't get rid of it."

For decades, the bar with the smoke-stained ceiling and red banquettes has been serving cocktails along with chasers of anonymity to DC power brokers. Here, people in the know come to meet, talk, and drink just a few steps away from the White House. While it's recognized that many a political player is a regular, the list remains off the record, no doubt part of its appeal.

"We don't advertise our guests," Wood says.

The art and coasters might offer a few clues. Caricatures of political players fill the walls at the bar. Drawn by well-known political cartoonists, the black-and-white ones from the bar's earlier days hang in the back near the fireplace. There you will find the likenesses of Jimmy Carter, Ted Kennedy, and Richard Nixon, created for the bar in the 1970s. Original sketches that showcase current times fill most of the rest of the bar, and a combination of old and new caricatures hangs over covered Table 51, the most private table in the place. When seated at the tucked-away booth, guests sip bourbon

beneath a crack pipe–wielding Marion Barry and an unamused-looking Vladimir Putin decked out in military garb. New pieces are created every year or so, and works from its large collection are rotated in and out regularly.

Off the Record's coaster collection gets updated more quickly than the wall art to reflect current political trends, elections, and personalities. Three political cartoonists—Pulitzer Prize winners Ann Telnaes and Matt Wuerker, and accomplished artist Kevin "KAL" Kallaugher—were commissioned

by The Hay-Adams to create the popular items that guests often take home. The items are so well liked that new designs are continuously being drawn. All the coasters share the same design on the flip side, a Wuerker cartoon of longtime former bartender John Boswell, behind the iconic bar with the smoke-stained ceiling and all in the background.

"We started this in 2014," Wood shares. "We started with four, and four became eight. Then eight became eighteen and then twenty. With the latest collection, we should be at twenty-four."

With new coasters in hand, guests can slip out to the street from a door near the bar's entrance, adding to its not-for-attribution appeal. For those who don't want to exit in a hurry, the Top of The Hay offers one of the city's most iconic views. Live shots and election night results are often broadcasted from the space. Up here, those in the know look out over the city while others who value not being looked at remain in the bar below.

HIRSHHORN MUSEUM AND SCULPTURE GARDEN

Hilary-Morgan Watt's job at the Hirshhorn Museum is to let people in through the side doors. Every day, Watt and her team prop them open with Facebook, Twitter, Instagram, and YouTube. They use social media to offer the public a peek at the art and artists featured inside the contemporary art museum's curved walls. Sometimes their posts, videos, or chats even inspire the person on the other side of the screen to take the relationship to the next level—walking through the actual main door.

"I hear many stories about how someone has seen photos of their peers in the space—walking through the galleries, posing in the sculpture garden, or with a favorite work of art—and then felt more comfortable," says Watt, the Hirshhorn Museum and Sculpture Garden's digital engagement manager. "I think more people than before are starting to feel welcome in museums, and I believe social media helps drive that. Helping people to feel welcome and making art accessible is the core that drives my work."

The Hirshhorn prides itself on being among the earliest of the Smithsonian museums to embrace the revolution. "Social media accounts had existed since before I joined the team at the Hirshhorn," she states. "But I was the first full-time person they hired. It had previously existed as one part of the many duties for the press officer. So when they hired me, it was a strategic decision to scale up their efforts and really think about digital audiences."

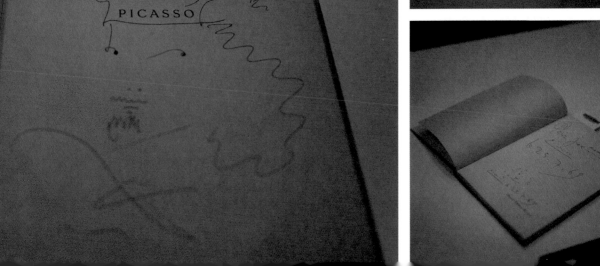

It's been an engaging ride ever since. Watt holds up the museum's wildly popular 2017 exhibit as a digital outreach highpoint. "Our team decided to share visitor testimonials on social media," she says. "During one of my interviews, I spoke with a pair in their early twenties named Emily and Jordan. Emily had been a [Yayoi] Kusama fan since she studied art in high school. She brought Jordan along. This was his first experience in a museum of any kind. He was just in awe from exploring the show. I really treasure sharing that moment with them."

Sometimes a sparkly guitar makes the moment. "When you see a bunch of photos of a female rock star surrounded by glittering gold curtains in a museum, and then you read that caption . . . detailing how you could step into the museum and find one musician playing a note over and over again," she shares, referencing the "Woman in E" performance piece by Icelandic multidisciplinary artist Ragnar Kjartansson, "it sounds so wild, who could resist?"

Watt and her team often find inspiration in the galleries and in the garden, although ideas inhabit every turn here. "I also like to bring my laptop downstairs to work and observe audiences a little bit more," she says. "I like to see which works draw them in."

Set on the fourth floor, the Hirshhorn's library fits that draw-them-in bill. Pun intended. Open to the public by appointment only, the library originated with Joseph Hirshhorn's large personal collection. Among its sixty thousand plus treasures are catalogues, monographs, and rare periodicals. Several Picasso books inscribed and signed by the artist to his friend Hirshhorn dazzle. The volumes reside in a small room off the side of the library not readily accessible to the public and also house other treasures like Yoko Ono's "A Box of Smile," a shiny black plastic box with a mirror inside.

"Not only did Picasso autograph the book, he signed it with a doodle," Smithsonian Institution library technician Rebecca Bruner says as she points to the original sketch of a bearded man with curly hair and a wavy hat.

A doodle worth a thousand words and at least as many likes.

IPPAKUTEI TEA HOUSE
AT THE EMBASSY OF JAPAN,
WASHINGTON, DC

A short path behind one of Embassy Row's Modernist façades leads walkers back through centuries. At the footpath's end stands a traditional Japanese tea house surrounded by a rock garden that catches stray pink petals from a crepe myrtle in the right season. It is both picturesque and captivating, at odds with the traffic just a few feet away on Massachusetts Avenue.

Built in 1960 behind the current Japanese chancery to commemorate the centennial of the ratification of the Japan–US Treaty of Amity and Commerce, *Ippakutei*, or the "Tea House of 100 Years," communicates history, tranquility, and an air of quiet strength. The garden, the house, and the ancient tea ceremonies hosted within it offer embassy guests a chance to immerse themselves in Japanese history and culture.

Each element of the tea house design reflects the experiential nature of the ceremony, with the architecture and ritual working in unison to support it. A twenty-seven-square-inch opening serves as the formal entrance, which guests crawl through after removing their shoes on the porch and being greeted by their host. "It shows that you are humbling yourself," says Mitsue Morita, public affairs counselor for the Embassy of Japan. "When you come here, everyone is equal. You leave rank and worldly values outside. All guests are equal in the tea house."

Inside there are two distinct rooms. The first, which is the smaller of the two, carries the name *Buka-an*, meaning "tea room of dancing flowers." This name was chosen

because it also sounds like the last name of the president who welcomed Japan's first diplomatic mission to the United States in 1860. Blue-and-white checkers adorn the wall in the larger room, adding color to the otherwise austere décor. In both rooms, everyone sits on their knees on the floor, if they can, throughout the ceremony led by the tea master. Some of the masters who serve tea at Ippakutei study at the Chado Urasenke Tankokai Washington DC Association downtown (see page 153.)

Japanese craftspeople built the tea house in Japan, disassembled it, transported it to DC, and then reassembled it at the embassy. Architect Nahiko Emori designed the structure, which is often cited as one of the best examples of a tea house outside of Japan. It incorporates all the historic elements of the form including a rack outside attached to the low roof overhang. The rack is intended as a place to hang one's sword while inside. This function of Ippakutei is no longer used.

JAY CARPENTER'S STONE-CARVING WORKSHOP

Jesus Christ, Kermit the Frog, and Amelia Earhart look on as Jay Hall Carpenter works. The well-known figures watch as Carpenter forms others from clay, talent, and skill in this soaring space that he also created with his hands.

Carpenter designed his home studio after spending twenty years as a sculptor for the National Cathedral. So it's not terribly surprising that a subtle church-like energy fills the workshop, with its high ceilings, religious sculptures in varying stages of completion, and a cross made from the space surrounding the window placement on the back wall. The light-filled workspace can neither be seen nor detected from the front of the house he shares with his wife and daughter. From the street, it looks not unlike any of the other homes in his suburban Maryland neighborhood. A low wooden gate painted red leads to a nondescript side door, the studio's entrance and portal to the world of his art and process. A world he built.

"I designed the studio, and then we had an architect draw it," a soft-spoken Carpenter says. "I kept telling him, 'No, you are changing it; this is what I want.' I had a contractor I was going to let do the whole thing But I had to fire him halfway through."

The Silver Spring-based artist completed the job that sounds as though it was carved from the earth up. "The ground level was right at the top of the concrete, so we had to remove all this dirt and form up the walls," he explains.

Intention led the process and design. It even informed decisions about heating. "When we built the studio, there were five massive oak trees," he says. "The wood from

it was stacked up in rows that completely covered the backyard. I gave half of it away, and we heated the studio for five years with the other half. That's why we put in a wood stove."

Among the items he built in the studio are a sauna for clay, a moveable stand for works in progress, and a platform where his daughter, Fiona, likes to sit when she comes to visit him or is sitting for her portrait sculpture.

His craft really is many in one, with studio design among them. His approach to art was passed down from artist to artist, as it was to Carpenter from his mentor at the cathedral, Frederick Elliott Hart. "Fredrick Hart was a huge influence on me," he says. "He had studied with Felix de Weldon, who studied with [other masters]. And so that nineteenth-century French academic tradition was handed down in that way. Also studio process, mold making, clay preparations, all the armature building and studio constriction, as well, were all part of my training."

Carpenter became interested in sculpting as a somewhat lonely high school student at the St. Albans School, located on the grounds of the cathedral, which had not been completed at the time. He would watch the stone carvers through the window. "I became infatuated," he says.

Eventually, he worked up the nerve to ask for a job. "The first year, I swept floors, built shelves, ran errands, and did things like that," he says. "But I sculpted a gargoyle on the weekends, brought it in, and showed it to the master carver. He liked it and carved it for the building. That was my first sculpture. It was 1976. I was in tenth grade. It's a gremlin committing suicide."

The gargoyle adorns the west façade of the building. It is one of hundreds of pieces he has sculpted for the cathedral—the famous Darth Vader gargoyle among them. He points to his sculpture for the crypt as his favorite. "The tympanum at the cathedral are the big artists' statements," he shares. "I really wanted to do one, and there weren't any left, or so I thought. As it turned out, the entrance to the crypt had an available spot."

After two decades sculpting for the cathedral, he decided to go out on his own. Now he spends about half his time doing religious pieces and the other half doing other commissions like the sculpture of Jim Henson and Kermit the Frog for the University of Maryland. Jane Henson and Kermit came to the studio during the process.

"I had the Kermit that was used for still photography," he says. "They brought it down on one of the visits. And to send it back, I had to put it in the regular mail. They said don't insure it; don't describe it on the package; just send it. They didn't want to tip off thieves. Now it's in the Smithsonian."

Other artists, like graphic novelist Gareth Hinds, occasionally also spend time working in the studio Carpenter created. "Jay said he wasn't using his drawing board very much, and he invited me in to use his space," says Hinds, a Takoma Park resident who worked on his *Iliad* here.

The characters from the classics that Hinds drew now hang out with the other famous ones that have been brought to life in this studio.

JOHN A. WILSON BUILDING

Josh Gibson's office looks like an eBay Washington, DC, memorabilia search brought to life by magic DC statehood fairy dust. It's a one-room, single-curator, DC council fandom museum of sorts hiding behind the government-issued door of suite 17 tucked away on the ground level of the John A. Wilson Building.

It is not even close to an exaggeration to say that photos, patches, cards, newspaper clippings, postcards, maps, pendants, and other DC keepsakes, souvenirs, and collectables cover almost every prime inch of wall space. Buttons of DC politicians through the years include such gems as "Barry Backs Carter," "Sterling Tucker for Chairman," and "Re-elect Councilman Wilson Ward 2 He gets things done." Others advertise the candidacy of Linda Cropp or declare "I was in Washington DC when the hostages were released." A blue pin with the words "Washington for Washington for" written in a circle creates the feeling that the message is without end.

The DC political buttons started it all. "I found out from a local antiques store that they'd received a large lot of DC political pins," says Gibson, director of communications and public information officer for the Council of the District of Columbia. "I went to check them out, picked through them very carefully . . . then was given such a reasonable price for the handful I had selected that instead I just bought the whole lot."

"Whole lot" is also an apt description of the treasures he unearths to fill the space. What he has amassed speaks to recent DC history as well as DC's beginnings. "I love the handful of pre-retrocession maps of DC," he states. "DC was created out of parts

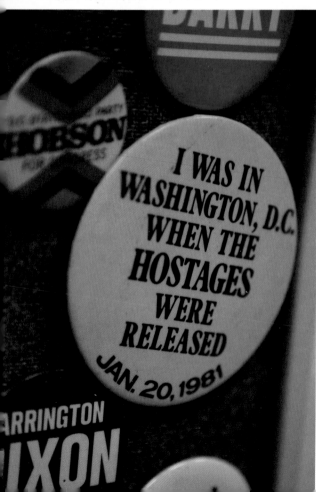

I WAS IN WASHINGTON, D.C. WHEN THE HOSTAGES WERE RELEASED JAN. 20, 1981

of Maryland and Virginia, but in 1846, in somewhat sketchy circumstances, Virginia took its part back. That's called retrocession. So, pre-retrocession maps are the ones that show DC as it was meant to be: a full diamond without the current bite."

Gibson cites his "signature collection" as another current favorite, with autographs of Marion Barry, Walter Washington, Sterling Tucker, Anthony Williams, Chuck Brown, and, a recent addition, Boss Shepherd. Maps of the Wilson Building pile up on a table near the far wall. He points to room 503, the not-open-to-the-public Chairman's Conference Room, which has posed and candid photographs of all past council chairs as well as

DC voting rights–themed political cartoons by Herblock and Clifford Berryman.

Voting rights is a theme that touches many of the items in the office downstairs, too. One of the more emotionally charged pieces in his collection is a photograph of a ninety-eight-year-old lifelong District of Columbia resident voting for the first time ever in 1964 at a Janney Elementary School polling place. His son, in his sixties at the time, looks on as he gets ready to do the same. "We didn't have home rule [yet]," he says. "He is ninety-eight years old going to vote for the first time not because he wasn't interested in voting but because there was no vote in DC [until then]."

KENILWORTH PARK
& AQUATIC GARDENS

Frank Hamilton stands between the two tanks that line the sides of one of the long, narrow greenhouses that L. Helen Shaw Fowler built. The National Park Service gardener reaches down in the water to pull out a tuber sprouting stringy roots that look like over-cooked rice noodles from a plastic colander submerged in the shallow tank. Holding the young plant in one hand, he uses the other to point out various parts of the plant as he describes the techniques he uses to get the dark brown morel-like root to bloom into a Monet-worthy water lily—the very same techniques perfected by the woman who put up this hothouse in 1913.

"We learn right here on the job from the older gardeners," says Hamilton, who has tended to the water blossoms at Kenilworth Park & Aquatic Gardens for some fifteen years. "That's how we really learn what to do. It's passed on down to us."

The Kenilworth oral gardening tradition began decades ago, when Fowler shared her aquatic plant knowledge with an NPS gardener named Fred Lundy. Lundy worked for Fowler when the vast Northeast DC wetlands property still was Shaw Aquatic Gardens, a private water garden started in the 1880s by her father. When Fowler, who took over the business in 1921, sold the garden to the government in 1938 to save it from being filled, a few Shaw Aquatic Gardens staff members, including Lundy, stayed on, becoming park employees. "She had a big workforce that her father put together," explains Ranger Elizabeth White. "And it was a diverse workforce. They were all different income levels. They were black and white people working together. Right after the American Civil War, for him to put together a diverse team together was significant."

Deeply connected to the place that she fought long and hard to keep but ultimately could not, Fowler lived in a small house on the property until her death in 1957. Living here put her in close proximity to the new and continuing team caring for the almost nine picturesque acres of floating flowers. Historical records tell of her not only imparting gardening wisdom during this period but also giving tours to visitors. "She essentially teaches those maintenance rangers what to do," says White. "And then that knowledge is passed down from ranger to ranger. It comes directly from Helen Fowler."

Walter Shaw purchased the current Kenilworth Gardens shortly after he returned from fighting in the Civil War. He planted and tended to the water garden on the willow-dotted marshlands as a kind of therapy. "Her father came back from the war quite traumatized," says White. "He lost his right arm in the American Civil War. He came out here and started the garden for a sense of recreation. I believe he suffered from PTSD. He starts to plant these gardens. His daughter would follow him out to the ponds. They share that experience. Eventually he realizes this can be a business."

A very successful business, as it turned out. More ponds were dug over the year to grow more lilies, lotuses, and other aquatic plants. Shaw began to experiment with hybridizing water lilies with great results, a development that took the place from personal oasis to personal oasis slash business. One particular variety he developed in 1900 became one of the world's most popular hybrids at the time. He named the hardy deep-rose-colored bloom with a yellow center for his daughter. The hybrids launched the business in many ways, but it was Fowler who took it to great heights.

"She really considered these plants to be her family," says White, who added that Fowler was a young widow whose only child died. "She was the one who built the greenhouses that we are in right now. In 1913, when she started to take the business on, she took out a loan [to fund the hothouses]. Within one year after they took out that loan, these greenhouses were paid off."

Fowler traveled the world in search of exotic aquatic plant varieties and created catalogues to sell them. Tapping into another one of her artistic gifts, the lily whisperer illustrated the pages with her pretty

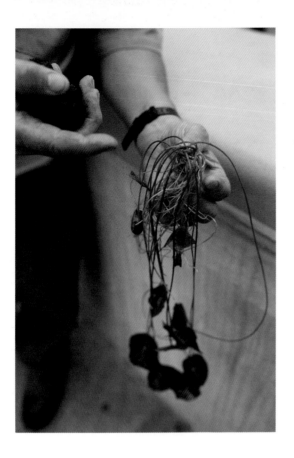

watercolor paintings in addition to penning the engaging copy that dazzled with flair and marketing prowess. "It is a satisfaction to know that a water garden actually increases the value of your property," Fowler writes in her 1932 catalog. "If your grounds are not as lovely as you desire them to be. If you want to live surrounded by a new degree of loveliness and if you want the most of nature's beauty for the lowest cost and effort then water gardening is for you."

Stories still circulate of Fowler making customer housecalls. "I remember a visitor coming in and saying, 'She dug my pond,'" White says. "Even in the catalog, people would write reviews, like they do on Amazon; they would say, 'Well, she came out to my yard in DC and dug a pond for me.' That's how dedicated she was to getting ponds in every person's backyard."

When Fowler pulled up to a job site, she would be sitting in the driver's seat. The multitalented entrepreneur holds the distinction of being the first woman in Washington, DC, to obtain a commercial driver's license. "I created quite a stir peddling pond lilies in a gas wagon," Fowler has been quoted as saying.

She had an impressive set of accomplishments for anyone at any time, especially during an era not exactly known for its professional opportunities for women. A memo she wrote indicated the ponds generated a profit of more than sixty thousand dollars in the five years between 1922 and 1927, a significant sum for the time. By 1935 the garden spanned nine acres, boasted forty-two ponds that hosted about half a million plants among them. During its heyday, thousands of people flocked to the gardens on the weekends.

Along with Fowler's gardening secrets and the memorable flowers she left behind, the original greenhouses she built remain at Kenilworth and are used season after

season. Not typically open to the public, the three concrete-and-wood buildings shelter the tubers through their journey from tank to outdoor ponds. It's a delicate process that starts in February and requires time in each of the three houses. With each move, the plant is transferred into a larger pot until it is ready to be planted outside so it can be grown to peak, which comes midsummer. By the time the plants reach the last greenhouse, picture-perfect flowers in lilac, violet, soft pink, and an almost glowing version of white poke out of the water. The lily pads resting on the water's surface grow in a rainbow of greens from light to dark, complementing but not overshadowing the round flowers that somehow feel reminiscent of stars if they were to shine in the daylight. Some of the foliage even hides a muted red coloring along its veining or underside.

Hamilton, checking the water temperatures and level, looks around and nods. A bit of sunshine filters through the panels in the slanted roof. "They are one hundred years old, and they still work well," he says of the structures he knows so thoroughly. "I wouldn't change a thing."

LINCOLN MEMORIAL UNDERCROFT

Deep below the Lincoln Memorial, footsteps take on the sound of a lone hiker kicking up dust in the woods. Each step on the uneven dirt floor pierces a profound quiet that drifts through the cavernous space. Outside noises rarely register here. Not even hints of the tourists above taking selfies with the sixteenth president pierce the monument's massive undercroft filled with towering concrete columns and arches high overhead. Moving through it all is like exploring a forgotten underground treasure, a rarely seen monument of its own to structure, art, and architecture that in places feels as history laden as the one that it supports directly above.

"Remember, this was swamp that was filled over time," says National Park Service historic architect Audrey Tepper as she stands in the undercroft. "In order to keep the building stable, they had to go down far. When you think about how elevated the memorial is and that it's really on flat land, in essence you have built a temple on a mountain. This is the mountain."

It's a subterranean mountain in two parts with its base about forty feet below the popular attraction. The section under the actual iconic monument itself and also the more structurally crowded area under the cobblestone plaza give off a Hogwarts meets Luray Caverns with a dash of deconstructed cathedral kind of vibe.

"You have the dichotomy of a very raw space down below and this incredible marble temple above," says Tepper. "The contrast is really interesting. People don't realize what lies below."

Initially, the foundation of the monument, which opened in 1922, did not reach down as far as it does today. Soon after the memorial was built but before it opened, it became obvious there was a problem. "They had to come after the fact and dig a foundation down to bedrock," Tepper explains. "It was a major structural failure. I don't know whether it's true or not, but [some people believe that] the dirt you see [in the undercroft] is a result of them having to dig down to reinforce the raised terrace. It would make sense. They had a contained space, and they couldn't get the dirt out, so they kept it in here."

Work on the Greek Revival memorial started in 1914 and took eight years to complete. During that stretch, construction workers, presumably the people who poured the concrete, left their marks on the historic project. Graffiti done in black charcoal, some of it rather artistic, remains on a handful of the pillars in the undercroft. About fifty drawings in total, the images speak to the style of the day with some of the male figures wearing bowler hats and at least one decked out in a top hat and handlebar mustache à la the Monopoly Man. Many have speculated that a figure that appears repeatedly is the job foreman. Sporting a brimmed hat, work boots, and overalls over his big belly, the man presumed to be the boss stands with his hands in pockets while smoking a pipe. Inexplicably, a small duck rests on his back.

"It probably was a way workers passed the time," Tepper says, adding with a smile that the little dog wagging its tail is her favorite. "We, of course, discourage graffiti, but it is pretty amazing."

Not far from the dog, on a pillar with several figures, there's a caricature of a woman in profile done up in heavy makeup. Guessed by some to be actress Gloria Swanson, a cigarette dangles from her lips. Presumably unrelated, to the left of the smoke that drifts up from her drag is a horse's head. The other female figure captured down here is a bit cruder in rendition and subject matter—a woman from behind bent over and unclothed except for a pair of ankle socks.

"I assume it's a woman," Tepper says.

A few games of tic-tac-toe also remain frozen in time on yet another support. Plexiglas shields cover some of the doodles, but most remain in good shape just as the unnamed artists who drew them all those years ago left them. "Charcoal lasts a long time if you don't rub up against it," Tepper says.

Catherine Dewey, National Park Service chief of resource management, knows of at least one case years ago of a descendent of a worker who came to the Lincoln Memorial saying that his relative worked on the monument and drew some of the figures. "Most of them have passed, since it has been almost one hundred years since it was built," Dewey says.

Graffiti hidden under memorial or historic places like this appears to be a phenomenon limited to the Lincoln Memorial.

"I haven't seen this elsewhere in the park . . . or on other projects I've worked on in DC," says National Mall and Memorial Parks supervisory park ranger Ted White.

"Or on historic sites worldwide," Dewey adds.

"On a construction site, you spend so much time there that you kind of want to leave your mark," Tepper theorizes. "You work for years on this project, and it is bittersweet to leave it behind. Or perhaps the motivation is that they were fooling around one day and wanted to draw a flapper girl."

A reinforced portion of the ceiling moves the focus away from the vintage graffiti upward toward the man upstairs. The iconic Daniel Chester French statue of Honest Abe on his chair rests atop this spot. The extra support has held him in place all these years.

Several coal chutes along the walls of the undercroft run all the way up to the top of the monument near where he sits. They were part of a rudimentary and not completely thought-out mechanical system to heat and thereby better preserve the two oil portraits there—one on the north wall and one on the south wall. "It was intended that they would be able to heat those walls very gently," Tepper explains. "There also were old furnaces here. I don't think they ever worked to capacity. It was abandoned

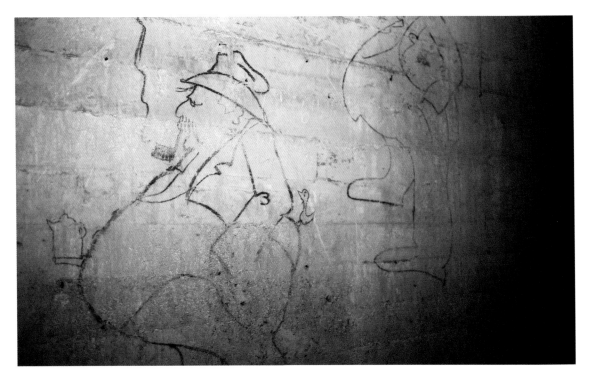

pretty early on. Black soot was generated from the coal that was dumped up on this lovely white marble."

As the tour of the undercroft moves on, the air becomes humid and dense when entering the space that stretches below the plaza. Long stalactites hang from the ceiling. Water droplets fall from the spiky formations every few minutes, sometimes hitting the crude walkway left over from tours once conducted under here in the 1970s and 1980s. Stalagmites that look like fried eggs form on the wooden planks referred to down here as, wait for it, "Abe eggs."

"It is calcium carbonate dripping in from the mortar above," Tepper says as she explains the appearance of the typical cave-dwelling formations. "There are cracks in the surface, not major structural cracks, but enough for moisture to get through. It may be cast stone, but it still has some of the same qualities as a cavern."

Tours haven't walked through the space in decades. As of this writing, a plan was underway to create a new viewing window to offer a peek of the underground world below the monument stalactites, chutes, scribbles and all. Until then its secrets remain concealed quietly below the surface.

MARVIN GAYE PARK

Bricks from Marvin Gaye's razed childhood home at 12 60th Street, NE, grace the back wall of the Riverside Healthy Living Center. Tales of the first moments of his professional career still hang in the air. Memories have faded of a time when his voice, with its four-octave range, filled the space then called the Crystal Room, a nightclub that opened after sundown and closed when the rest of the city sat down to breakfast. Outside, DC's longest park, once named for a local slave-owning family and later nicknamed for its drug infestation, now bears the name of the murdered Motown star, the same man who once worked this room until the sun came up over the park.

Marvin Gaye Park, not unlike its namesake who was notoriously abused by his father when he lived here, suffered greatly until about fifteen years ago, when neighbors began reclaiming the 1.6 miles of winding green space. During a five-year period, volunteers removed thousands of hypodermic needles, millions of pounds of trash, and almost a hundred abandoned cars that clogged the park and stream located in far Northeastern DC. In 2004, as the cleanup was underway, Washington Parks & People purchased the abandoned Deanwood nightclub to launch the Riverside Center. It now

serves as a healthy food incubator space, cafe, bike repair station, and community class and program space. It also contains an indoor seedling nursery to support its open-to-all urban farm around the corner.

"People come here to grow, to volunteer, and to learn," says the center's farm and food hub manager Ashleigh Mitchell while standing among the wheelchair-accessible rows at the Marvin Gaye Community Greening Center she helps run. "It's a place to gather and be."

It's also a place that shines with community-forward art. Mosaics illuminating a series of names line the curb outside the center on Foote Street, also called Marvin Gaye Way. The instructions for the project were simple. Honor someone you consider a local hero by adorning his or her first name on the edge of the street. All included on the sidewalk are African American and have strong connections to the neighborhood, the park, and the local Marvin Gaye legacy or to all three, as is the case for lifelong Deanwood resident Earl Simpson. Two stars, one blue and one white, flank his name written in maroon cursive.

"Earl regularly brought his keyboard down to the park to lift up the memory of Marvin Gaye, whose musical debut as a

teen living in the neighborhood had been all but forgotten before he and the Riverside campaign launched the drive to change the name of the park from that of a slaveholding family named Watts," tells Steve Coleman, Washington Parks & People executive director and president. "As he played at park events and cleanups, dressed in his Scoutmaster's uniform, Earl would adapt the lyrics of Marvin Gaye and other Motown greats to tell the story of the park, the stream valley, and the drive to reclaim them for all to enjoy."

Nearby, the name Chantelle celebrates the five-year-old girl who led the community in a celebratory walk of the entire park trail following the massive cleanup efforts— believed to be the first time in eighteen years that the entire park could be walked. "The trail had been obstructed for a long time by illegally dumped construction debris after the closing of the garbage dump that had long clogged the mouth of the stream valley opposite the National Arboretum," Coleman says. "As she led the community across the last stream bridge into the end

of the park at Lady Bird Meadows beside the corner of Minnesota and Nannie Helen Burroughs Avenue, Mr. Simpson was waiting with his keyboard. He serenaded everyone with 'Celebrate' and 'I Heard It Through the Grapevine.' "

Stories attached to the other names on the street include tales of park advocates like Murphy, a returned citizen who helped lead the movement to reclaim the Riverside Center and the Marvin Gaye Amphitheater; John Campbell, the community barber who convened the Save Our Park group in his shop; and Nannie Helen Burroughs, a pioneer and visionary in African American women's education, who founded and ran the much-lauded National Training School for Women and Girls next to the park.

Mosaics celebrating all of them join other local heroes with similarly inspiring stories whose names now pop with color and pride beside Marvin Gaye Park. Their legacies, along with his, are now permanently cemented to the neighborhood and all it holds dear.

MCKEE-BESHERS WILDLIFE MANAGEMENT AREA SUNFLOWER FIELDS

A bright yellow spell falls over thirty acres of open land off River Road every summer for two weeks. It quietly lifts hundreds upon hundreds of sunflowers out of the ground and toward the sky, creating something closely resembling magic for those who come to experience the rows of flowers in full beautiful bloom.

When the sunflowers do open, visitors flock to the McKee-Beshers Wildlife Management Area in Poolesville, Maryland. At just about any given moment of daylight during peak bloom, people from near and far can be seen setting up tripods, painting at easels, taking wedding photos, running after toddlers, piloting the occasional drone, meditating, and wading through the tall flowers. Later in the season, mourning doves and other animals also flock to the nine fields, the intended purpose of the site. McKee-Beshers is a public hunting ground run by the Maryland Department of Natural Resources as part of its wildlife management program. Hunting season does not happen until well past peak and the last sunflower-seeking shutterbug has long gone.

MERIDIAN HILL PARK/
MALCOLM X PARK

A tragedy brought Steve Coleman to Meridian Hill Park for the first time.

It was January 1990, and Washington, DC, was the murder capital of the country. In the middle of the day, gunfire stole the life of a seventeen-year-old neighborhood boy named Ricky Magnus. Magnus, one of four teenagers and one of a total of fourteen people murdered in DC that weekend, wound up dying in the arms of Coleman's housemate, who had run out to try to help him when she heard the shots.

"This was at noon on Dr. King's birthday," says Coleman, Washington Parks & People executive director and president. "He was playing on the street and [was] shot in a driveway. The police came out and put up the yellow tape. They said, 'Go inside. Lock your doors. Don't talk to strangers. Don't go out at night. And, whatever you do, don't go into the park. Day or night.'"

Coleman and his neighbors didn't know what to do, but they also didn't believe going inside was the answer. So they decided to organize a community meeting for the following evening at Coleman's home, violating the police request to stay indoors after dark. More than fifty people showed up. Amid the discussion, someone in the room shared a story about a group of grandparents in Southeast who started a crime patrol with an interesting approach.

"They had two rules," Coleman says. "The first was that you couldn't carry anything that looked even a little bit like a weapon. The second was you had to say hello to everyone no matter what they looked like or if you were afraid. Especially if you were afraid."

Soon after the meeting, Coleman and his partner on the newly formed safety patrol walked up the stairs to enter Meridian Hill, also called Malcolm X Park, for their shift. All they had for protection were their orange hats identifying them as patrol members and a CB radio that quickly lost its signal. "We walked down this path," he says from the now-thriving park located on the place Thomas Jefferson thought should be the prime meridian. "There was broken glass. There were dime bags on the ground. There was graffiti on the benches. But we also felt drawn in. There was a bit of a moon out. We didn't know it had been a Native American sacred ground. We didn't know it had been an African American theological seminary. We didn't know it had been a Civil War Union army hospital or that this hilltop was the beginning of higher learning in this city. But there was something about it that pulled us in."

As they were drawn in on that cold, dark night, they discovered the park was empty. Well, almost empty. Surprised by the stillness, they began walking farther inside. They noticed two shadowy figures in the distance. "We remembered the rule that we had to say hello," Coleman says. "We walked up, and said, 'Hi, we're part of the neighborhood crime patrol.'

There was a pause before the man answered. 'Welcome, I am Reverend Morris Samuel. Welcome to Meridian Hill.' He was the mayor of the park. He had been coming here for thirty-six years. He proposed to his wife under a cherry tree at the bottom of the park. He was here the night Dr. King had been assassinated. He saw the fires consume part of the city below, but even then he found peace in the park. He was here when people dying of AIDS would find solace here in their last days."

It's at this point that Coleman's narrative gets wrapped up with the narrative of the park just as so many other people's stories and moments have throughout the years. Coleman and Reverend Samuel began a friendship and partnership to return the park to the neighbors along with Howard Coleman, the man walking in the park that night with the reverend. (Although they have the same last name, the two men are not related.) They worked with the leadership of advocate and activist Josephine Butler, a founder and chair of the DC Statehood Party, who also led Washington Parks & People until the time of her death.

Together the group planted hundreds of trees here, planned programs, dreamed, and created. Samuel, Butler, and Howard Coleman have since died. "I think of Morris," Coleman says, his hand resting on a full-grown tree he believes is the one the two men planted to replace the original tree under which his friend proposed to his wife. A spark of peace seems to transfer from the tree to Coleman when his hand meets the bark. "I learned so much from him and from Josephine and from Howard. I get to carry them with me wherever I go. I go all over the world sharing what we learned and what I learned from them. Places they never dreamed of going."

Steve Coleman carries on their memory and their commitment to the park and the city through his actions and by sharing what he calls the invisible park. Shadows and pieces of the "invisible park" can be detected throughout Meridian Hill for those who know where to look. Some harken back to when the intent was to place the French embassy on this hilltop—hence the French influence on the design. Another plan included placing the vice president's residence in what now is the Josephine Butler Parks Center overlooking the park. Neither obviously panned out.

"Notice how there are these spaces between the benches," he says. "That's because they wanted this to be lined by sculpture." Although sculptures don't bedeck the green space, several do exist in and out of sight in the park. The area where kids now are drawn to play originally was supposed to be a playground.

"I'll show you a hidden thing over here that not everyone sees here," he says, and begins walking to a statue concealed by trees on a path near the Sixteenth Street side of the park. "Here she is. Our late treasurer called her the tribute to abused women everywhere."

Her name is *Serenity*, a sculpture by Josep Clarà. The public did not respond kindly to the statue of a seated woman when she was unveiled in 1925. A petition circulated asserting that her thighs were too big and that she should be removed from the public eye. Pockmarks on the marble came courtesy of the hammers in the hands of her

critics, the first recorded act of vandalism in the park. Her nose is gone. So are one of her hands and a few of the nails on the remaining one. She's been scribbled on and has had paint thrown on her over the years.

"I think of it as a triumph," Coleman says. "She is here. Like we all are a little bruised and battered. Like we all are."

In full view, the park's statue of *Joan of Arc* by Paul Dubois stands as triumphantly as her sister *Serenity* sits quietly. The women

of France gifted Joan to the women of the United States shortly after US women won the right to vote. French women would have to wait until 1945 to be enfranchised. The only female equestrian statue in the city, it's a copy of the one at the Reims Cathedral in France. A teenage Joan sits on horseback at the end of the top level of the park, which, although it is only half the length of the top, looks equal because of the forced perspective used to create it.

Just beyond Joan, a cascading waterfall connects the upper and lower sections of the park. Touted as the longest of its kind in North America and inspired by the famous fountains of Italy.

A pedestal beyond the fountain hides in an overgrown shrub. It once served as the base to Noyes Armillary Sphere, known to generations of neighborhood residents as "the sundial," and kids often climbed on it. In 1970 the National Park Service removed it for safe keeping. "Ironically, its removal led to its misplacement," Coleman says. "Despite a story that circulated for many years that it had been stolen and melted down, Friends of Meridian Hill/Parks & People launched a search for the sphere on Valentine's Day 1992. On that very day, a park service curator called to report that he had the cherub that had been at the center of the sphere."

Stories such as this one are everywhere throughout the park. Even the walls tell them. Pebbles from the Potomac River create the depth and texture of the walls. Coleman recalls how his friend Morris would bring a towel to place over the low wall behind Joan so the bump of the rocks would not leave an imprint on the reverend's arms when he leaned on them to look out over the city.

"You can pass the park a million times and never notice what you are really looking at," Coleman tells. "Here's a wall, but it's so much more than a wall. What you are looking at is the first large-scale use of exposed aggregate on concrete anywhere in North America. It goes way beyond that. They took it to the level of art. See how it has the unexposed aggregate framing it. Notice how, other than the unexposed part, you don't see any of the cement. What you see is the pebbles. That was an incredible level of artistry. What they wanted was to evoke a Renaissance form in the style with a modern American material. But in a way, that evokes an Impressionist, a Pointillist, image in it when the sunlight hits the multicolored pebbles to form a single hue out of the many colors."

"Which is kind of like this neighborhood," he adds.

And this park.

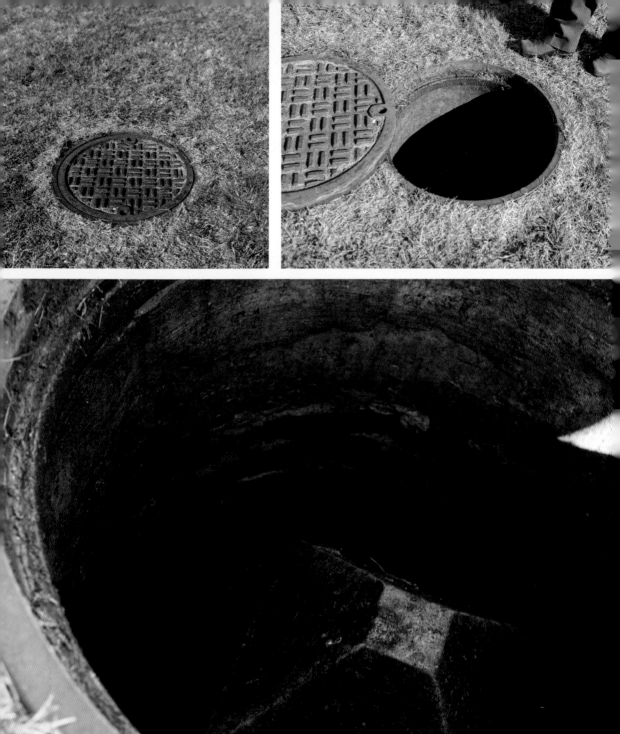

MINI MON

A mini Washington Monument hides underground a few feet away from the real thing. The concrete replica, which sports the street name "Mini Mon" but officially goes by "Bench Mark A" or the "Elevation Obelisk," was placed there in the late 1880s by the US Coast and Geodetic Survey to measure how the monument was settling into the ground over time. For a while in the 1950s, it went by the nickname of "baby monument," but unlike the structure itself, that one did not stand the test of time.

"My understanding is that it was placed there by the US Geodetic Survey in order to calculate the long term amount of in-ground settling of the Washington Monument," the NPS's Eric Martin elaborates. "It is somewhere in the neighborhood of 0.01 of an inch every few years."

Listed as thirteen and a half feet tall and three feet wide in the Cultural Landscape Report and the National Register, the Mini Mon is a "true obelisk geometrically," according to Martin. Still, the copy of the Washington Monument can only be found in its maintenance hole by those who know where to look and those who have the authority to remove the cover that conceals it from the throngs of Mall-goers who walk past and over it each day. Alas, even exposed it's hard to see down to the base of this no-longer-in-use underfoot oddity.

MUSEUM RESOURCE CENTER–VIETNAM VETERANS MEMORIAL COLLECTION

Boxes the color of a bright cloudless sky line the long aisles formed by open shelves, a slightly darker shade of blue, and stretch up toward the ceiling of the brightly lit modern warehouse-type structure. The boxes climb so high that staff members, who wear blue archival gloves when they work here, must use electronic lifts to access the top ones. The long, same-colored rows create a visual uniformity, which at first registers as startling and then, after an adjustment period, almost comforting. After a while, a feeling of familiarity arises. It's a sense that this place has grown to be unintentionally reminiscent of the Vietnam Veterans Memorial itself, the iconic black wall that gave birth to this place, its mission, and all of its blueness.

These emotionally charged, specially created blue rows occupy only a sliver of the football-field-size National Park Service Museum Resource Center in Landover despite the fact that they house almost a half million items—objects that have been left at the Vietnam Veterans Memorial. Since the Wall was dedicated in 1982, people who come to see it have been moved to place "offerings" at its base, a phenomenon not seen at other memorials or monuments before or since.

"At first it was kind of spontaneous things," says Vietnam Veterans Memorial Museum curator Janet Folkerts of the early objects left at the wall. "A lot of times it was something they took out of their pocket. Things written on the back of receipts or business cards. A picture they had been holding on to for a really long time. They were smaller, more personal objects at first."

As time passed, the offerings began to vary. Baseball gloves, cigarettes, combat boots, medals, beer cans, paper cranes, barbed-wire wreaths, helmets, pieces of uniforms, fishing rods, games, Vietnam War–themed folk art, flags, guitars, sake sets, Mass cards, dog tags, motorcycle gas tanks, POW bracelets, bibles, birthday cards, newspaper clippings, Zippo lighters, poems, and hundreds and hundreds of photos are just some of what has been left over the years.

"It was always the photos that got to me, especially as you were cataloguing this stuff," says Joanne Westbrook, Museum Resource Center supervisory curator. "These guys look like babies, and you realize the photos are probably here because they aren't here anymore. These guys were maybe younger than I was when I first started working here. I think about how it was probably the last picture taken of them alive."

Initially park rangers collected the offerings that were then stored in a maintenance facility. In 1984, the regional curator at the time made the decision to start an ongoing collection. Ever since, every evening, park rangers walk the length of the wall to collect what has been placed against it. About once a week Folkerts comes down to the Mall to sort through them and take them back to Landover, where they are catalogued, preserved, and stored in the blue boxes created just for this collection. The park service now keeps only objects that have context, which translates into approximately five hundred new pieces a year. A box for cards is left on the plaza during holiday time—many of them also become part of the collections.

Each piece helps shed light on the life of a person on the Wall and what his or her death has meant to others. They also share the many individual journeys of grief that sprung from the Vietnam War, like those of Eleanor Wimbish, whose son William "Billy" Reed Stocks, nicknamed Sparky, was killed in Vietnam. Wimbish lived in Glen Burnie, Maryland, and would come to the Wall all the time to leave things for her son, including long letters she wrote to him. They are among the first items in the collection.

"She would come all the time for Veterans Day, his birthday, Christmas, and Easter and leave him letters," Folkerts says. "She would usually write the letters, and her husband would put them in this plastic seal so they wouldn't get damaged when they left them. She left things probably for the first ten years or so, and then it started to get less and less. As she aged, she probably was less able to travel. She doesn't leave anything anymore. I think she has passed away. I don't know if her family comes or if he has other relatives who visit."

In one of her letters to her son, Wimbish talks about the day the monument was dedicated. "The day was unseasonably warm and sunny when we arrived in Washington, DC," her letter reads. "We got out of the car and started walking toward this memorial. I could feel the pull toward this black wall, yet my feet didn't want to move. I was so scared. I was afraid I would find your name on the black wall, and I was afraid some mistake had been made and your name had been left out. I reached for your father's hands. They were ice cold. His face was pale. He looked at the black wall and then at me and said, "What a waste. All these men and women died and for what. For fighting a war that they had no way of winning."

Wimbish's handwritten words and Sparky's memory now live in perpetuity among the blue boxes.

NATIONAL ARCHIVES AT COLLEGE PARK, MD, XRF ANALYSIS LAB

X-ray fluorescence (XRF) spectrometry sounds like something from the pages of a vintage comic book. With its boxy base reminiscent of a 1970s TV camera minus the lens, cylindrical red and orange light, and mechanical arm–like extension, it even looks like Marvel drew up the blueprints. But looks can be deceiving, which in many ways is why the National Archives owns the highly specialized instrument.

When focused on important historical papers, the XRF sees beyond what even the most well trained eye can. Housed in its own lab on the archives' massive College Park campus, the machine gives chemists readouts on the makeup of inks, dyes, and photographs. The information guides them in deciding the safest ways to preserve the item without ever having to take a sample or disturb it in any other way. Understanding the chemical backstory of a yellow flourish on a hundreds-of-years-old family tree or the blue calligraphy on a Revolutionary War certificate means the staff knows what the document can and cannot withstand when it comes to conserving it.

Archives chemist Dr. Jennifer Herrmann demonstrates the XRF on a facsimile of an actual document she has analyzed, a colorful family tree going back generations. These precious family heirlooms often were the only documentation one had to prove the relationship to a deceased soldier for pension purposes. Once something is sent to the government, it becomes part of the permanent record.

The archives houses a sizeable collection of family histories and original art for this reason. The XRF aids in the preservation of the collection, some of which has sustained damage through the years. Knowing how to proceed with preservation can be critical. Herrmann points the x-ray on a small area of red before explaining how the XRF aids in the process.

"Here we have an energy of excitation for mercury, iron, and calcium," she begins. "So we know that this red pigment has mercury, iron, and calcium. Based on what we also know about historical objects, iron is contained in everything because so much of the earth's crust is made up of iron-containing dirt. Calcium also is something we would typically find in anything that has passed through the conservation labs, because calcium carbonate is added as a buffer. It keeps the paper stronger and keeps it [safe] from acid attacks. Which then brings us back to mercury. We don't put mercury in things. So therefore we know that this is cinnabar. This is mercury sulfide."

The instrument can also "see" through lamination and provide insights into how a document or photograph might respond to sunlight exposure, conservation processes, and other conditions. "We can use the XRF specifically to analyze the photos," she says. "And based upon what metals are present, we can say that you can probably leave this in full sun on display forever and it would be fine. (Of course, we would never do that, but it's an idea of how stable it is.) Or, we have to tell them please don't ever look at it again. Keep it in the dark."

The archives is a relatively new agency founded in 1934; many of the items it keeps have been through less than ideal conditions for long periods of time. "The archives didn't open to the public and didn't start bringing records in until the thirties," says Miriam Kleiman, archives program director for public affairs. "So you are getting records that have been in attics and garages and less-than-ideal conditions. The archives was the first government building with air conditioning in DC. And, remember, DC was a swamp."

Occasionally, Herrmann is called on to study presidential signatures from the early days of the republic. Just as with the pension documents, these items come through the lab with the purpose of determining a conservation plan. The archives doesn't authenticate these types of things because the chain of how it got there is known when it comes through the lab. But that doesn't

mean that the XRF can't provide valuable data about the items.

"We would take a spectrum, and with the presidential signature, they would all be iron gall ink. Presidential signatures would all be iron gall ink," she explains. "So I would look for the iron signal, the potassium signal, and the sulfate signal. Then I would say this is iron gall ink. Most of the time we would know it would be, but sometimes we want to double check before treatment, because iron gall ink is really interesting. Nobody really knows its chemical structure. We know there's iron, we know there's potassium, we know there

is sulfate, but there's also an organic part of it. Some iron gall ink is incredibly stable, and other iron gall ink fades. So there have to be differences."

What the XRF cannot measure is the emotion that goes along with being in the presence of a letter composed by George Washington's hand.

"I have analyzed George Washington's signature, Thomas Jefferson's signature, Abraham Lincoln's signature," she says, and smiles. "Every time I see their signatures, it's like I've never seen it before. It never gets old."

NATIONAL BUILDING MUSEUM ARCHIVES

Nancy Bateman sits on her knees on the carpeted floor of the National Building Museum's well-kept archives. Using both hands at once, she carefully pulls out a specially crafted shallow drawer to reveal a dozen timeworn shoes. Not one among them makes a pair with another. The same holds true for the thirteen other more-than-a-century-old mismatched shoes also found beneath the floor of the historic building prior to the museum's 1985 opening.

"There was a British tradition of hiding shoes for luck in a building or house," Bateman, the museum's registrar, explains while holding the drawer open. "It's a superstition. To protect against bad things happening, you'd put shoes beneath a building."

A hat and a pair of mittens similarly were uncovered along with the shoes during the restoration work completed to ready the building for the museum. "It is believed that shoes, mittens, and hats, which retain the shape of the human body even when they aren't being worn, are good luck charms," says National Building Museum's chief preparator Hank Griffith, who adds that this is why shoes get tied to the back of a couple's car after a wedding ceremony.

The old lucky charms are among the thousands of objects stored in the museum's onsite collections. Each item catalogued here either relates to the art of American building or to the Pension Building itself, the museum's home that dates back to 1887. "Most people don't know we are a collections museum," says Curator Chrysanthe

B. Broikos. "Obviously, we don't collect buildings."

What is collected essentially boils down to everything but the building. Think architectural plans, photographs, documents, drawings, bricks, models, building fragments, and a range of tools from the architectural, carpentry, and building professions. There even are stacks of building toys including original sets of Lincoln Logs, Erector Sets, and Tinkertoys. Museum archivists also collect keepsakes from the many inaugural balls that have taken place in the Grand Hall since the first one held here after President Grover Cleveland took the oath of office. No matter the subject matter, everything is meticulously labeled, stored, and ordered.

"I always say I have a master's in being organized," jokes Bateman. "We have about 250,000 items. If I put one away in the wrong drawer, I would never find it again."

Some of those meticulously organized treasures, like the photographs of Robert C. Lautman, have a strong DC connection. The renowned American architectural photographer made a name for himself capturing the gleam of many prominent local buildings, the National Cathedral and the Pension Building among them. The museum is the keeper of about thirty thousand items from his storied career. Vintage cameras and fragile glass plate negatives can also be found in the large section of the archives dedicated to building photography, where his collection resides.

Far from the photography collections, at the opposite end of the archives, a foam model with significant pedigree rests on a shelf. Its creator: Frank Gehry. The world-renowned architect designed it for a 1988 exhibition at the museum entitled *"Sheet Metal Craftsmanship: Progress in Building."*

The completed structure based on his model stood more than five stories high. Fashioned from foam core, metal pins, and glue, its significance and artistry far exceed the simple materials used to create it.

"It was meant to be a working model, not a final presentation piece," Bateman explains. "However, even in its rough form, you can see the elaborate design and genius behind the architecture."

Pieces like the Gehry model illustrate the intention driving the National Buildings Museum collections. "An art museum's goal is to have the final product," says Bateman.

"We never will have the final product. We have everything else."

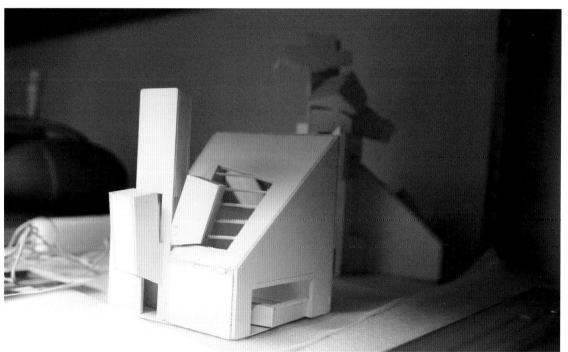

NATIONAL INSTITUTES OF HEALTH (NIH)

National Institutes of Health Clinical Center

FADE IN

INT. NIH CLINICAL CENTER—LATE MORNING—ESTABLISHING

Highly secured even-numbered floor of hospital.

Large windowless space. Drab color palette of cinder block gray, industrial tape silver, and plywood beige offer little for the eye until a swath of bright yellow with black lettering appears. Camera moves in closer until the words hazardous exhaust can be read.

The hum of mechanical systems plays in the background.

A door opens. Footsteps.

The setup screams spy flick. Its purpose speaks volumes.

Despite the fact that it drips with thriller motifs, the National Institutes of Health Clinical Center interstitial spaces are more documentary subject matter than potential action flick fodder.

Packed with wiring, ductwork, communications lines, air filters, and other utilities, the hospital's even-numbered floors, or interstitial spaces, contain the systems that keep the hospital running and safe, while the odd-numbered floors are dedicated to patient care. The separation means that most building-related problems can be fixed, changed, adjusted, and monitored without ever having to enter a patient's room.

"Basically, they built a separate floor for every floor in the building," says Craig Rodgers, the chief of hospital engineering and facility services, NIH Clinical Center, as he walks through one of the spaces. "The beauty of that is that if you decide you want to change or repurpose something, all the work is in here. You don't disturb anyone. The old part of our building is not like that. It is like an old hospital. Every time we do something, we shut down a whole hallway."

The interstitial floor above the highly contagious Ebola unit takes on the added job of containing airborne contagions, in part by being engineered to respond to airflow in all potential situations. "If the power goes off, these things shut down," Rodgers explains, motioning toward spring-loaded dampers that close the system during an outage. He also notes that the hospital was built with 100 percent redundancy and has enough generators on hand to supply the entire building twice. "What you don't want is to have the supply continue and the exhaust stop when the power is out. Then the room becomes hot, and the air pressure pushes out and affects everyone outside of the room."

Stainless steel ductwork, sealed light fixtures similar to those installed on submarines, and a special coating on the flooring add to the list of design adjustments that help keep air pressure and hazards in check. Even with all the safeguards, the patients' experience is kept in mind. "It's not like a box," Rodgers notes. "There are windows and things like that so you don't feel like you are in a cage."

The in-between floors also address less toxic but still problematic issues that come with operating a large building. "Believe it or not, there are a lot of leaks in hospitals," Rodgers says. "Let's say that your drain leaks and it's coming from the next floor. If they get to it quickly enough, before it goes down, you can contain it all in the interstitial space; whereas, if you were at a regular hospital, you would be leaking several floors down."

FADE OUT

Scene Two

INT. NIH CLINICAL CENTER

BASEMENT—MIDDAY—WIDE ON ROOM

Large basement storage unit filled with medical supplies behind what appears to be fencing. Low ceilings and fluorescent lighting. A wooden baby's crib can be seen behind the gate protecting the equipment against the back left wall. Blue cots in stacks catch the eye in the otherwise colorless scene. Plastic-coated manuals are clipped to the gates.

Interstitial spaces help protect patients within the hospital. What appears to be a well-stocked storage room off a basement corridor is part of a detailed plan that lets NIH doctors and nurses treat people beyond the limitations of those walls. In the event of an emergency or disaster in the area, the

Cots/Beds (Ped.)
Medical Supplies
House Supplies
General Supplies

Clinical Center can deploy a contingency hospital expanding its capacity by two hundred beds. Much like an army field hospital, it can be set up quickly in an open space like a gymnasium or even outdoors if necessary.

Packed with cots, cribs, IV poles, bandages, hygienic supplies, gowns, and other medical and emergency equipment, the secured room is a just-add-water mobile medical unit. (Medications would be dispensed from a different part of the hospital.) "We have enough supplies to set up a 250-bed hospital," explains Captain Antoinette Jones, patient representative, NIH Clinical Center, and part of the commissioned corps officers and facilities management team that manages the contingency hospital.

Discussion to ready and store a "pop-up" hospital on the campus began after September 11. The field-hospital-in-waiting maintained here was the result. Staff like Bernard Harper, chief of the materials management and environmental services department, NIH Clinical Center, check it regularly by inspecting, replacing, and rotating expired or compromised items. Easy-to-follow assembly manuals illustrated with pictures hang from the gates and are clearly labeled, as is everything else. "We wanted to make sure that, in a crisis, a person has step-by-step instructions. That's why we took the photos," says Jones, who is also a registered nurse.

It's an efficient plan as well as another real-life spy thriller plot device hidden away at NIH. From the basement up to the spaces in between, the Bethesda-based medical research center is apparently ready for just about every possibility, including a closeup or two.

CUE MUSIC
FADE OUT
THE END

9:30 CLUB

James Brown took the stage at the 9:30 Club seven times during his legendary career. Each time, the forebearer of funk proved to audiences how he earned the title of "Hardest-Working Man in Show Business." But before Brown worked the crowd, he first logged some serious time under what could be dubbed the hardest-working hairdryer in town. A rider in Brown's contract specified that a professional hooded dryer needed to be on site for his use. After renting one for Brown's first shows, the decision was made to buy one solely for the "Papa's Got a Brand New Bag" singer and songwriter. Even now, years after Brown's 2006 death, the nightclub holds the old-school beauty parlor–style workhorse in high esteem.

Although the likelihood that the Godfather of Soul ushered his hot pants through the delicate cycle in the nightclub's laundry room is slim to none, many others who have passed through the space gratefully take advantage of the unexpected amenity. The backstage laundry room is popular with many a road warrior who find themselves with a tour stop at the 9:30 Club. Headliners higher up the food chain also get to admire the mural on the ceiling that adorns the octagonal VIP dressing room, best studied from the sleek built-in black bunk beds.

THE FABULOUS JAMES BROWN PLAYED
9:30 CLUB SEVEN TIMES!

WE GOT SO USED TO HAVING THE
LEGEND AROUND THAT WE ACTUALLY
BOUGHT THIS HAIR DRYER (FOR HIS
USE ONLY) FOR WHENEVER HE CAME
THROUGH.

THE DATES HE PLAYED THE CLUB:
6-10-99 - 05-26-01 - 02-25-02
12-13-02 - 12-20-02 - 03-03-04
12-28-05

The Shaw club began its life in 1980 as the gritty Nightclub 9:30 in a back room of the Atlantic Building at 930 F Street, NW—note the street address for the origin story of its numeric name. It outgrew the space and reopened in 1996 as the 9:30 Club at 815 V Street, NW, where it remains today. Especially during its early days, the nightclub developed a reputation for showcasing emerging bands before they hit it big. In addition to Brown, acts that have played the club include the Ramones, the Go-Gos, The Police, Nirvana, R.E.M., Bob Dylan, the Beastie Boys, Adele, and Smashing Pumpkins, who headlined the first V Street show.

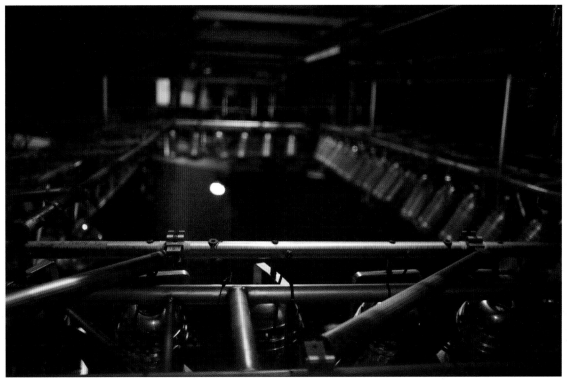

POTOMAC BOAT CLUB

With the white star on a worn red background underfoot and the steady motion of the water ahead, even the most devout land lover may hear the call to row standing on the dock of the Potomac River Club. A private Georgetown rowing club, the 1908 Craftsman-style boathouse sits at a place that offers its members many different views of DC, all of which can be absorbed from the same spot at the same time. Look to the left and through the arches of the Key Bridge, and the Kennedy Center, Watergate, Washington Monument, and Roosevelt Island frame the river. To the right, nothing but nature, water, green, sky, and land.

"From here on up, you can be in British Columbia," says Cal Sutliff, a member who first started rowing from PBC in 1954, when he was a student at Arlington's Washington-Lee High School. The school's crew team still rows from PBC and is the only high school to do so. "There's no development."

Being on that deck is not just about looking ahead. "You are standing where rowers you have respected for years have stood before you," says Courtney Farber, a rower who trains at the club. "It's a magical place." One that requires considerable attention to maintain.

Members like Sutliff volunteer to keep the club and its boats running, clean, and in good condition. The age of the clubhouse coupled with flooding, weather, and some years of neglect have provided challenges. So in 2014, volunteers established the Potomac River Boathouse Foundation to preserve the simple yet elegant structure designed by the same firm responsible for the Old Executive Office Building.

"It has a real Southern feel," Gretchen Ellsworth, president of the foundation and longtime member, says while standing on the second-floor porch overlooking the river. Rowing machines in lines take up much of the two-story ballroom behind her. A workout and hangout space for members, Olympic champions among them, the room also holds a long history of hosting dances, concerts, and parties over the years.

"My senior year in high school, my girlfriend was the 'crew queen' at a dance here," Sutliff recalls.

Ellsworth points out a part of a simple latch system in a ceiling beam once used to hold back a piece protecting the musicians' gallery so a piano could be hauled up there. An accomplished rower, she also is

responsible for many of the archival photos displayed in the club that showcase women rowers. Women were not allowed to join the club until the 1970s, although now about half of active rowers are women, says Ellsworth, who joined in 1995 after taking up the sport following her kids' rowing crew at Woodrow Wilson High School.

"A lot of master rowers get to it through their kids," she states.

Just as the water whispers to its loyal members like Ellsworth and Sutliff, so does the building itself. The original dark wood locker rooms and trophy-filled member lounge make it easy to imagine the early days and why so many have been drawn and continue to be drawn to it.

Like the club itself, its view is strictly for members only.

PRESIDENT LINCOLN'S COTTAGE

On a sweltering DC day, seventeen-year-old Sofia Ohanian stands in the shadow of the summer home where President Abraham Lincoln drafted the Emancipation Proclamation. The then high school senior releases a deep breath before starting a discussion about "the box" with her peers, who are seated at a picnic table in front of her.

"So you already know that I want to lock myself in a box," Ohanian tells the group, some two dozen teen activists from around the world chosen to participate in the weeklong Students Opposing Slavery International Summit on human trafficking. "There will be a time clock. And people will try to buy me out before time runs out. The idea is to model the debt bonding system. But in the end, they won't be able to get me out because, for slaves, there's no way out."

Immediately, the others respond with encouragement and suggestions about everything from where to put the box to the best social media outlets to spread the word about the box. (Ohanian has her eye on the National Mall, but if she can't obtain the appropriate permit, she says that she'll settle for the busy corner near her DC school's entrance.) As the day goes on, the rest of the teens share their plans for bringing awareness to modern slavery, the topic they have gathered to learn about during the special program that takes place every summer on the quiet Petworth hilltop.

President Lincoln's Cottage launched the Students Opposing Slavery summit in 2013 as an extension of its modern abolitionist mission. Both a historic site and a nonprofit organization, it works toward continuing Lincoln's legacy through its programs and its social justice approach toward historical preservation. So when staff uncovered receipts showing that Mary Todd Lincoln bought cocoa matting carpets for the cottage, in actuality a thirty-plus-room Gothic Revival summer estate, they made the decision to purchase rugs similar to those that were used when the Lincolns lived there for three summers from 1862 to 1864. But finding the most historically accurate carpet was not the only consideration in their search.

"One thing that we did, which is not often done in the historic preservation world, is we figured out that we didn't know where the carpet was coming from," explains President Lincoln's Cottage external communications coordinator Jenny Phillips. "We didn't know if it was ethically sourced. So we started this cocoa matting campaign to replace the carpet with ethically sourced certified slave-labor-free carpet. We actually are taking Lincoln's principles [into consideration] and putting our mission and what he probably would have wanted over historical accuracy, which not many historic houses do."

Much of the house can be toured, but a few hidden aspects within it speak to its history, its calmness, and its various incarnations over the year. A beam in the private staff library is signed with the name of architect John Skirving. Previously, it was believed that he had a very limited role in the design of the home, originally constructed beginning in 1842 for George Washington Riggs.

"They thought originally that he only did the veranda," Phillips says. "But when they found this beam, they thought it showed that he had more of a fingerprint on the house."

The Riggs family, along with enslaved individuals, lived in the house until 1850, when they sold it to the federal government. It has been government owned ever since. In the attic, the remains of the rooms where the enslaved people lived still can be seen. Papers and objects from the cottage's previous lives also fill the attic. The original cottage doors are located here as is a dusty framed piece of an April 30, 1940, newspaper found in the wall during renovations. There's also a rate card from when the place was the Anderson Guest House in the early 1900s. The four-dollar-per-day charge is crossed out and changed to five dollars a day.

In the basement, the remains of a dumbwaiter-type elevator used to haul kegs up the first floor is all that is left of the period in the 1970s, when the house was the Lincoln Lounge for retired soldiers who live on the grounds. The cottage sits on the 250-acre Old Soldiers' Home, now officially called the Armed Forces Retirement Home. A retirement campus for members of the armed forces, the home includes hilly grounds with fishing ponds, a golf course, and at one point its own power plant. The cemetery here is the precursor to Arlington National Cemetery. Lincoln witnessed soldiers being buried here almost daily when he lived here and often talked with the wounded and newly freed enslaved individuals.

"He spent many a day meditating out here," says Christopher Kelly, an Armed Forces Retirement Home spokesperson.

A statue of General Winfield Scott, the man responsible for the Old Soldiers' Home,

also stands on the property, full with green hills, winding paths, nesting birds, roaming deer, and wild-growing Queen Anne's lace. "Scott was the commanding general in the Mexican American War," Kelly explains. "He got war reparations from Mexico, and he took that money and went to Congress—there was no veterans' administration at the time—and said that he wanted property for his soldiers to be able to retire and live on. Lore has it that the statue is facing that way so he can keep an eye on Congress." Another story of activism and activist in the social justice thread unifying the many aspects old and new that belong to President Lincoln's Cottage.

PRESIDENT'S SUITE, RONALD REAGAN WASHINGTON NATIONAL AIRPORT

A dash of imagination carries this art deco–kissed room back in time to when it belonged to Franklin Delano Roosevelt and was a place for the thirty-second president to work and hold meetings as a crew readied his plane outside. The President's Suite on the ground floor of the original 1941 Washington National Airport terminal still has terrazzo flooring with an inlaid zinc medallion as it did in FDR's day. Also stored within the suite's walnut panel walls is the lore associated with the period that predates *Air Force One*, when commercial aviation was shiny and new.

"President Roosevelt would park his airplane right here and come in right here," says Mike McElwee, airport operations duty manager, as he gestures toward the runway from the operations duty office attached to the suite. "I imagine it was a quiet place for him to be while he was working."

A special conference table that accommodated Roosevelt's wheelchair is long gone, although a series of original brown leather couches do remain in the waiting area where guests would be escorted in for their appointments with the president. "They are like a museum piece behind those little stations," says McElwee.

The suite also allowed Roosevelt, the first president to fly for official business while in office, an easy path to and from his aircraft. "Since FDR was in a wheelchair, this was an easy and convenient place for the Secret Service to take him," explains Andrew Trull, Metropolitan Washington Airports Authority spokesperson. "He would have direct access onto his airplane while being rather inconspicuous about boarding."

SIXTH & I HISTORIC SYNAGOGUE

These walls don't need to talk. They tell stories. They also crack jokes, make political predications, and can even hum a few bars. The autograph-filled walls that line the back stairwell of Sixth & I have a lot to say.

Sometimes it's talk about friendship and admiration, like when Kelly Osbourne signed her name with an arrow and heart pointing toward Joan Rivers's signature, or how Rachel Maddow placed her name followed by a heart with an apostrophe before Michael Moore's John Hancock. Other times it's food banter, like when Giada De Laurentiis scribbled "Spaghetti is love" in orange ink. Or it's Wally Lamb acknowledging the soul of the space by writing "Shalom from Wally Lamb" or Rachel Bloom leaving the distinctly Jewish dis "Suck it Christmas." There's also Alan Cumming's self-portrait, Brené Brown's flower, and Valerie June's lipstick kiss along with signatures, doodles, and musings of the hundreds of people who have taken the stage at the historic synagogue turned cultural center slash community synagogue.

"The Wall of Fame is our effort to get everyone who performs and speaks here to leave a little piece of themselves here at Sixth & I," says Jackie Leventhal, the chief brand and content officer and the site's longest serving staff member, who has been bringing people back to sign the wall since 2007, not long after the tradition began.

Comedian Rob Corddry holds the honor of being the very first person to take Sharpie to cinder block after his 2006 performance at Sixth & I. The morning after his show, his name had been partly scrubbed off by a maintenance staff member who

RIVER CITY EXTENSION

EELS 2008

THE CHET ALSO

Michael Showa

I ♥ YOU

GUM

JEW!

WAKE STEVE UP!

mum

I think I'm converting!

ADAM LOWITT

ROB RIGGLE

Lewis Black

MICHAEL LOMBAS

JOHN CALVIN

Great is

Jonothin

Kozo

Michael Chabon
JOHN VANDERSLICE
AYELET WALDMAN

Hi! Hello! Bye!

XO ♥ OX
THE WATSON TWINS

Is this a schul, or a rock club?
Rob Tannenbaum is
NOT GOOD FOR THE JEWS

9.06

DAVID RABIN
GET JEWS!

FANG ISLAND

BLOOM ON!

SIT UBY

HADS

Samuel "Lachaim" Mugli

The Jews

MATT NATHANSON IS A 1/2 BREED. But LOVES HIS JEW-NESS!!

Cynthia B.

STRUGGLING MUSICIAN

NEW BROS

Abraham Heschel

thought it was graffiti. Since then, a vast collection of authors, politicians, musicians, and performers have left their indelible marks, including Toni Morrison, Tina Fey, Elena Kagan, Neil Patrick Harris, Khizr Khan, Oliver Sacks, Judy Blume, Gloria Steinem, John McCain, Mindy Kaling, Al Gore, Elie Wiesel, Carla Hall, Hasan Minhaj, Lewis Black, Matisyahu, Annie Leibovitz, and Idina Menzel.

The idea for the Wall of Fame came from Rory Zuckerman, a longtime volunteer who is married to one of the men who stepped in at the eleventh hour in 2002 to save the historic building from developers. "It was very simple really," says the children's singer. "I have a background in theater and was a touring recording artist playing at a theater. I don't remember where the theater was, but I remember outside of the dressing room that people who had performed there had started to sign."

All involved often marvel at the Wall of Fame, now so full that additional space soon will be needed. Leventhal reports how even if a very serious celebrity comes back to sign, he or she often will smile and let down their guard when they notice the name of someone that matters to them. The same holds true for many of the staff and volunteers when they walk through the hallway. Leventhal points to Tina Fey, who she booked, as one of the signatures with particular significance for the

institution. "I feel like she put us on the map in a way," she tells of the show that sold out instantly. "We kind of think about our author series before Tina Fey and after Tina Fey," she says. "[She] gave us a lot of legitimacy and street cred. I feel like that was a turning point professionally and personally."

Joan Rivers performed at the historic synagogue twice, the second time shortly before her death. Her sharp wit and intense kindness made a lasting impression. "The first time she was here, she thanked everyone and she shook everyone's hand," Leventhal remembers. "She could not have been more gracious."

The legendary comedian already had walked past the security desk and was almost to the street when she heard that a synagogue staff person had been hit on the

head when something in the green room accidently fell off the wall. "You heard this 'Oh my god, are you okay, are you okay?' " Leventhal recounts. "She literally stopped in her tracks . . . she's out the door. The limo is waiting outside. [The injured woman] was on the couch and kind of had her hand on her head. Joan went over to her. She asked what happened and how the person felt. She told her she should go to the hospital. You can't take it easy with head injuries. They can be very serious. She was taking care of her in such a motherly kind way. It showed everything about who she was."

SKATING PAVILION IN ANACOSTIA PARK

Humidity and the smell of lit charcoal fuse together in the summer air. Trophies topped with disco balls, boxes of cassette tapes, and computer equipment get placed on top of a folding table about to serve as a makeshift DJ booth. Laces get tightened, checked, and relaced. Kids, grownups, families, fans, and passers-by slowly come together to form a small crowd. The music starts, the conversations quiet, and the collective attention shifts toward the center of the outdoor roller rink. The last "Artistic Rollerz" show of the summer is about to begin.

For decades, neighbors and skaters have been drawn to Anacostia Park's skating pavilion and these weekend shows. Like the park around it, the open-all-summer-long rink is part of the National Park Service, making both admission and skate rental free for anyone with an ID and a pair of socks. The only roller skating rink in the entire park system, the large covered skating floor with open sides is something of a neighborhood institution, drawing people together for fun, community, spins around the floor—and the shows. Many who sit on the built-in wide concrete bench-like border that surrounds the rink remember a time in the seventies and eighties when hundreds would flock here every summer to watch and perform. The newest version of the

interactive performance takes that energy and legacy and mixes it with a welcoming vibe that includes a kids dance contest and lots of prizes for the youngest spectators and participants.

"I realized I was good at skating and thought maybe I can do this to be more involved with the city," says Diamond Gerald, a member of the Artistic Rollerz who goes just by Diamond in the skating world. She organizes the free shows and has been part of DC's robust skating scene since the late 1990s. "We don't get paid. We do it for the love of skating."

Interspersed with the contests and games, Diamond and the other members of the Artist Rollerz perform jumps, tricks, and flips during their choreographed routines. The group is made up of local skaters who range in age from twenty-seven to sixty-five. A ten-year-old junior member also rolls with them from time to time. Diamond, who also mentors young students, has traveled throughout the country and as far away as Japan for roller skating competitions and exhibitions. She often showcases DC's hallmark skating technique on the road.

"It's called a snap," says Diamond, who

grew up near the DC line in Capitol Heights, Maryland. "It's done with two or more people in a line. The one in front is doing dips or turns, and the other people follow while keeping the speed up."

"The DC style," she adds, "is very pretty."

THOMAS JEFFERSON MEMORIAL UNDERCROFT

Spending time in the circular undercroft of the Jefferson Memorial is akin to walking through a giant excavated sundial or a crude approximation of a sundial. Evenly spaced beams radiate overhead and underfoot, with columns running vertically between the spokes. The dirt floor and basic construction site–style lighting add a visual layer of unremarkable to the quite remarkable job the sunless chamber performs, supporting a marble rotunda overhead. In the reinforced center of it all is the exact place above where a bronze Thomas Jefferson looks out over the Tidal Basin.

"It's kind of the basement that people don't get to go in," says National Park Service historic architect Audrey Tepper. Much like any other basement, the allure is the opportunity to see what, if anything, may lurk below something known and not open to public. "These spaces were never really meant to be accessed. Still, it's an interesting space."

Not far from what indeed is an interesting space, Tepper and her National Park Service colleagues can hide away with the kinds of things typically stored in basements that don't belong to national monuments. Books, videos, slides, newspaper clippings, maps, and other media old and new fill the shelves and tabletops of the windowless staff library at the Jefferson Memorial. Here rangers can research and read about all things having to do with the many NPS sites on the Mall, including the iconic memorial outside.

TINY JEWEL BOX

The "tiny" in the shop's name gets lost among the vastness of its address, but its historic significance lives large in the memory of Jim Rosenheim. The Tiny Jewel Box CEO readily recalls a time when customers could stand in the middle of the shop, spread out their arms, and touch both walls. It was a time when the thought of outgrowing the moniker wasn't even a twinkle on one of the broaches sold by his parents at the antique jewelry store they had started almost ninety years ago.

"The store was so narrow, we had to have special cases made," Rosenheim says of the Tiny Jewel Box's five-foot-wide, twenty-foot-long original home on G Street, NW. "It was a breezeway between two buildings. It had no running water. My parents worked in that store for nineteen years."

Rosenheim began helping in that store as a child, making his first sale at the age of six, when he sold a fifteen-dollar ring. "This year was my sixty-fourth consecutive December behind the counter," Rosenheim tells.

Like his mother, who worked until she was ninety-one, he has no plans on ending his streak anytime soon. "I've never seen anyone in my family retire," says Matthew Rosenheim, Jim's son and Tiny Jewel Box's current president.

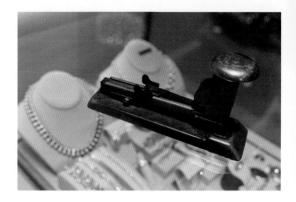

With this kind of work ethic in tow, the Tiny Jewel Box moved to Connecticut Avenue in 1956. It was the first of several addresses it occupied on that stretch of downtown, including one that formerly housed a grand Elizabeth Arden spa. Unveiled in 1914, the salon stood as Arden's second location in the United States and spoke to a time when effort was underway

to create a Fifth Avenue–type feel along Connecticut Avenue, according to Rosenheim. A few remnants from the salon days were hidden away in the basement of the building, which now has official historic designation, when the family took it over. Some of the items from the old Red Door days met with basement floods or the perils of time, but a pair of lanterns that framed the entryway survived.

A heavy old stapler at the store also serves as a physical reminder of DC days gone by. "It's the original stapler from my parents' first store," Jim Rosenheim says, adding that everyone knows not to remove it from its place of honor in his office. "I played with it when I was a kid. It's all metal. It works perfectly. It's the best stapler I ever had or ever used."

UP TOP ACRES,
THE FARM AT 55 M STREET

Some people talk to their plants to get them to grow. At Up Top Acres, it's the sounds of the seventh inning stretch, James Taylor performing live, and low-flying helicopters that lure the crops out of the ground or, more accurately, out of the roof.

The rooftop farm at 55 M Street, SE, has been growing watermelons, cucumbers, herbs, and other produce with the music of the city in the background since 2016. Overlooking Nationals Park, it's one of an increasing number of farms the company has planted with the goal of selling the local crops to the people who work and live in the neighborhoods below.

Up Top Acres cofounder Kathleen O'Keefe caught urban farming fever on a trip to Brooklyn. Hoping to replicate what she saw back in her hometown, the urban planner started throwing the idea around with her two Woodrow Wilson High School buddies, one of whom happened to be Jose Andres's personal gardener.

"We started talking to [Andres] about the idea, and he really liked it," says O'Keefe. "He helped us pitch the building that Oyamel is in. That was our first farm. After that, we could bring developers to the farm and show them what we meant."

O'Keefe and her partners purposely made Up Top Acres a for-profit endeavor rather than a nonprofit one. "We want to prove that urban agriculture is a viable industry," she explains. "That you really can grow in the city."

Considerably larger than the one on the restaurant rooftop, the Farm at 55 M Street was planted a year later. Their first head scratcher was figuring out how to get

250,000 pounds of soil on top of the building. The answer involved a crane, wheelbarrows, and a group of loyal friends.

"It took two full days," she says. "We had a crane that would bring up a super sack of soil. Each sack weighed a little over a ton. But the crane can only extend so far over the building. So what we would do was cut a hole in the bottom of the super sack. The soil would dump out. Then we had a chain of fifteen wheelbarrows. We'd take the wheelbarrow of soil, dump it at the end of the roof, and run back and get the next load of soil. It was a lot of soil."

"We have some really great friends," she adds.

URASENKE TEA CEREMONY ASSOCIATION OF WASHINGTON, DC (CHADO URASENKE TANKOKAI WASHINGTON, DC)

Downtown is working on its lunchtime routine. Car horns startle pedestrians gazing down at their phone screens, food trucks jockey for spots along the curb, and people balancing salads and to-go cups flood the sidewalks. Noise, crowds, and commotion define the show. Step inside a suite housed in a nondescript office building along a busy stretch of L Street and calm, quiet, and deliberate motions take center stage. Arriving here means keeping the chaos of midday on street level.

On the second story of 1819 L Street, NW, the Urasenke Tea Ceremony Association of Washington, DC, has transformed office space into a traditional tearoom for the purpose of studying the Chado Japanese "Way of Tea." Much like *Ippakutei*, Japanese craftspeople built the tearoom in Kyoto and then transported it to Washington in 2012. Within the carefully constructed space, Mioko Miller introduces her students, people from all walks of life around the city, to the ancient practice. Each movement of the tea ceremony is studied and practiced over and over again, with each practice leading

to deeper understanding and appreciation. Miller and the other four volunteer instructors at Urasenke also teach students the art of preparing the tearoom, the tea bowls, utensils, and the brewing of the tea itself.

"Many of my students call it their therapy," Miller says. The tranquil entrancing space and subject no doubt provide an attraction in a busy city like DC. "They look forward to the quiet moments."

The tea ceremony touches on many aspects of Japanese culture at once, including the kimono, calligraphy, architecture, pottery, and flower arranging. Miller, who began the study of tea at eighteen, observes a renewed interest in these cultural aspects and practice, one she refers to as a lifelong pursuit that always offers something new to learn or discover. "I started because my mother said so," she says. "Now it's different, people choose to do so."

Many new to the way of tea also appreciate its equalizing intention. "We serve everyone the same way," says Miller. "Through tea you see the best of the person."

US BOTANIC GARDEN PRODUCTION FACILITY

A two-acre government-run greenhouse in DC's Anacostia neighborhood, the US Botanic Garden Production Facility is where hundreds of orchids, cacti, and other flora live out the rest of their days after being seized by US Customs. There they are tenderly nursed back to health side-by-side thousands of other examples of plant life in this closed-to-the-public collection.

"Often what we are sent is so rare or endangered that it only exists in the wild," says US Botanic Garden plant curator Bill McLaughlin, who helps care for the living contraband sent there. "Sometimes we don't know what we have until it blooms. So you have to nurse it back to health and get it to successfully bloom. It can be years before we know what it is."

Equipped with thirty-four greenhouse bays and seventeen environmental zones, the production facility is one of a handful of centers around the country authorized to care for illegally transported CITES (the Convention on International Trade in Endangered Species of Wild Fauna and Flora) plants, one of the many jobs of the gardeners here. About seven miles from the Botanic Garden's public site near the Capitol, the 85,000-square-foot campus specializes in orchids, cacti, and succulents, which make up much of its CITES and general collection.

"There are collectors of plants just like there are collectors of art," McLaughlin explains. "And so there's a black market out there." More often than not, the traffickers

attempt to mail the items they smuggle. Starved of sunlight and water, the intercepted plants often arrive at the facility brown and desiccated. Nursing them back to health is only the start of the US Botanic Garden Production Facility's commitment to them.

"One of the conditions in the CITES program is that we have to agree to permanently keep this plant forever in perpetuity," McLaughlin shares. "One of the reasons . . . is they can [be called] in as evidence. It doesn't happen very often, but it can happen."

The dedication to the protocols goes well beyond the illegal imports' potential value to a court case. It also fully aligns with the Botanic Garden's overarching mission to shelter and propagate plants. Tens of thousands of aboveboard examples also are tended to and grown at the working facility right alongside those from the CITES program. Gardeners treat each item individually and have even been known to overnight pollen with other facilities to keep their charges strong.

"This [also] is where we house all the plants not on display uptown [on the mall]," says Devin Dotson, the garden's public affairs and exhibits specialist. "It's just like the archives at a museum. Our total collection at any given time is roughly sixty-five thousand plants. We are able to switch out plants when they are doing something interesting like fruiting or flowering. There are some things here that are being grown for upcoming seasons. One whole bay is filled with poinsettias for the holiday show."

The garden's infamous "corpse flower," officially named *Amorphophallus titanum* and notorious for its putrid smell, makes its home here when not being shown off for the crowds. Thousands of orchids, including ones named for each first lady, also live onsite, as well as a selection of prehistoric plant varieties. There are even a few carnivorous plants that once belonged to John Laroche, aka the Orchid Thief.

"Actually, I know the Orchid Thief," McLaughlin says of the man made famous by Susan Orlean's bestselling book of the same name. "He visited our old nursery some years ago. He was a character. He had a car packed with plants, and he wanted to do plant trading. We couldn't do anything like this now. But back then it was [different]. We have a pitcher plant his then-wife bred. He might have just given those to us—like a calling card. When I found out later he was the one taking the ghost orchids . . . I was blown away."

He goes on to note that the case illustrates elements of the underbelly of the plant trade. "We spoke his language," he adds. "There was a bond there, but everyone is aware that people take it too far. And that's how plants wind up being confiscated."

US CITIZENSHIP AND IMMIGRATION SERVICES: WASHINGTON FIELD OFFICE

Today is a special day, when the second-floor conference room at this local immigration services field office fills with about-to-be new Americans. People from all over the world sit in the first rows after devoting years to waiting, learning, and sacrificing. Today nineteen children take those coveted front seats. Their parents watch from the rows behind them, smiling, crying, and snapping photos with paparazzi-strength zeal as their children promise to "support and defend the Constitution and laws of the United States of America against all enemies, foreign and domestic."

Today the room with white walls and high-traffic gray carpeting explodes with bright color, capes, and characters. The blue of a pint-sized Batman mask, the red on Captain America's puffed-out chest, and the silvery white gleam of the headpiece worn by a young Audrey Hepburn circa *Breakfast at Tiffany's* seem to make the colors of the flag in the front of the room shine brighter, maybe even better or bolder.

Today is special times nineteen. Special times nineteen *plus* fun-size candy bars.

The annual Halloween-themed naturalization celebration hosted by the US Citizenship and Immigration Services Washington Field Office is a favorite office tradition.

For the past ten years, the Fairfax office has embraced the special October 31 ceremony with enthusiasm, decorations, and a bounty of candy for the costumed kids who come to put an exclamation point at the end of their family's immigration story. By setting up bowls on chairs next to their office doors, the staff who purchases candy for the day creates a high-yield trick-or-treat course in the hallways connected to the naturalization room. Many take the time to congratulate and shake hands with the pirates, ninjas, fairies, bumblebees, superheroes, and other newest Americans—the youngest among them two and the oldest, twelve.

Children's naturalization ceremonies occur several times throughout the year. Although technically only people older than fourteen must take the oath, these events mark the milestone for minors either adopted internationally or born to parents who recently naturalized. The list of birth countries of the kids reads as diverse as the makeup of the United States itself, with today's group hailing from Afghanistan, Azerbaijan, Bangladesh, Bolivia, Canada,

Democratic Republic of Congo, Egypt, El Salvador, Ethiopia, Germany, Ghana, India, Iraq, Israel, Morocco, Pakistan, Peru, Philippines, Singapore, South Korea, Uganda, and United Arab Emirates.

"You are all here today because your parents came to this country, and they worked hard and studied hard . . . or because your parents searched the world to find you," the group of nineteen kids was told. "You are now American citizens just like them. Either way, the citizenship we celebrate today is a gift to you from your parents, so please be sure to thank them. Thank them for all that they have done to make this day possible."

Small fingers ranging in size from tiny to growing preteen tightly hold the sticks of mini flags while they listen to speeches, instructions, and then pledge the larger version of Old Glory facing them. Some of the littlest ones need help walking to the front of the room when their names are called to receive their official certificates. A few also get an assist figuring out left from right so they can raise the correct hand for the oath. The grownups in the room along with the older children like Maria Cucho happily help.

Sitting between her proud parents in the waiting room before the big moment, Cucho takes a few minutes to read over the text of the oath that she already pretty much knows by heart. The nine-year-old's family moved to the United States from Peru when she was two. A lot of paperwork and a lot of waiting led them to Fairfax this Halloween. When asked what she is most excited about now that she is a citizen, without missing a beat she answers that it's being able to vote when she grows up. The articulate third-grader, who dons a black velvet witch's hat with a purple ribbon, later gives interviews in both English and Spanish before hitting the hallway for the trick-or-treating with the other new Americans. Her father looks at her lovingly and reports that tonight he plans on cooking his daughter's favorite dinner, filet mignon.

Many of the families sharing the experience today echo each other as they speak about the sense of excitement and relief that this day finally has arrived. They talk of gratitude, family, and love and finally being able to travel to see family in their countries of birth—something many have been unable to do during the long process. For a few precious hours on this Halloween afternoon, the struggles and challenges seem to melt away.

Talk shifts to watching scary movies, eating more candy, and another round of trick-or-treating—all three activities are included on Shabir Safi's to-do list for the rest of the afternoon. Born in Kabul, Safi arrived in the country when he was eight months old. Halfway between eight and nine this Halloween,

he receives his citizenship certificate with his father and uncle cheering him on in the audience. Even his Grim Reaper mask cannot conceal the boy's bright smile when he pulls it over his face to show off his costume.

Before heading home, Kara Lee pauses in front of a "Celebrate America" banner while her parents snap pictures. Dressed in a pink and green traditional South Korean dress, a nod to her heritage, the nine-year-old stands in front of the Statue of Liberty creating as near a perfect image as could possibly be constructed of what this day means—and has meant through the years—to so many. The photo-op-ready corner saw a lot of traffic today, as it undoubtedly does all year-round.

The afternoon is winding down. The halls empty as the winged and masked children filter out. The candy bowls are almost empty. Susanna Keller prepares to leave. She hopes her preschool-age daughter, Benedicte, whom she adopted from Congo, will fall asleep on the way home. The pair drove two hours from their Charlottesville home to be here today. Before they head back for another couple of hours in the car, the little girl with a witch's dress over her street clothes stops, backtracks to the chair where earlier she set down her neon green bucket overflowing with candy, and pulls out a lollipop. She takes a lick because today also is special times lollipops.

US NATIONAL ARBORETUM ORIGINAL ENTRANCE

Far away from the commerce and commotion of Georgetown, there is a spot in Northeast DC where M Street quietly becomes a dirt road. Here concrete barriers unceremoniously signal the place where the finished street ends and the overgrown foliage and gravel-and-trash-strewn portion takes over. It also is where those in the know who are willing to work a little for it can take in the original entrance to the US National Arboretum.

Through the fencing, barriers, and wild shrubbery, it's still possible to spy the long stone and wrought iron gates. What appears to be the insignia of the arboretum on a large concrete or possibly stone post almost can be made out from here, while the overall art deco feel is easier to appreciate despite the distance. At one time the pedestrian-friendly gates near where M Street and Maryland Avenue meet allowed neighbors, as well as those visiting by car, to pass through them with ease.

In 1992 the arboretum closed the entrance, citing crime as the reason. It was part of a move by the research facility and public garden known for its azaleas to make it safer, according to newspaper reports from the time. The gates remain locked despite a sharp decline in the city's crime rate since that time.

Recently, there has been a renewed push among neighborhood groups to reopen the M Street gates so they can easily access 446 acres of public green space. But for now, the closed-off gates remain a hidden reminder of what once was and what possibly could be for the arboretum.

ASSOCIATION OF JOURNEYMEN
STONECUTTERS

JULY 2
1850

LITTLE FALLS QUARRY
DISTRICT OF COLUMBIA
PRESENTED BY
TIMOTHY O'NEALE.

FRANKL
OF W
INSTIT

WASHINGTON MONUMENT

All fifty states, a handful of cities, a number of foreign countries, and a circa 1870 group identifying themselves as the "oldest inhabitants of the District of Columbia" occupy a little piece of real estate inside the Washington Monument. Over time, they have all become one with the interior walls of the 555-foot obelisk's winding stairwell in the form of almost two hundred individual commemorative stones honoring the first president. The tributes, which vary in size and scope, adorn the walls of the landing portions of the staircase that surrounds the elevator shaft. They also act as a history-rich distraction for those who have the rare opportunity and lung capacity to tackle the 898 steps it takes to get to the top—a climb that's been off limits to the public since the 1970s.

"The first commemorative stones were donated to the monument in 1849," writes Judith M. Jacob, a senior conservator with the National Park Service, in her study and catalog of the commemorative stones. "The original purpose for these stones seems to have been twofold. One was representative, whereby all 'States of the Union [were to be] properly represented' with a block of native stone and the state's name carved across the face. The second purpose was to aid in fund-raising. The Washington

National Monument Society initially planned to accept stones along with a cash donation. While records show that some stones did come with this extra donation, for the most part, it seems that stones were delivered without it."

States and the other groups that donated stones crafted commemorations as varied as the donors behind them. Some of the states even incorporated materials that showed off a trait or aspect of the place from which they hailed. At 320 feet up, Arizona is written in gold leaf across three pieces of petrified wood from the Chalcedony Forest. The Michigan offering, found at 210 feet, is done in silver and copper from a mine on Lake Superior. It tips the scales at more than two thousand pounds. Jade and bronze are the standout elements on the Alaska plaque, which can be found at the 450-foot mark not far from the observation area up top. The forty-ninth state dedicated its stone in 1982 on George Washington's 250th birthday, making it the second-to-last of the monument's 194 plaques.

New additions are a rarity, with the vast majority of the ones inside dating back to the years between 1849 to 1855. Back in the day, stones were shipped by rail, ship, and with the help of oxen, according to Jacob's research. A bit of state trivia can be picked up when taking in the stones, as is the case with the two that hang together representing the people of Utah. The newer one uses the name Utah while the older of the two says "Deseret," Utah's pre-statehood name.

The most recent stone was gifted to the monument in 2016 from the people of Ireland. "In honor of the many millions of Irish who contributed so much to the United States of America and their homeland," reads the plaque, which also commemorates the hundredth anniversary of the Easter Rising. There is no official word on how it got to town, but it does seem safe to say that livestock were not involved.

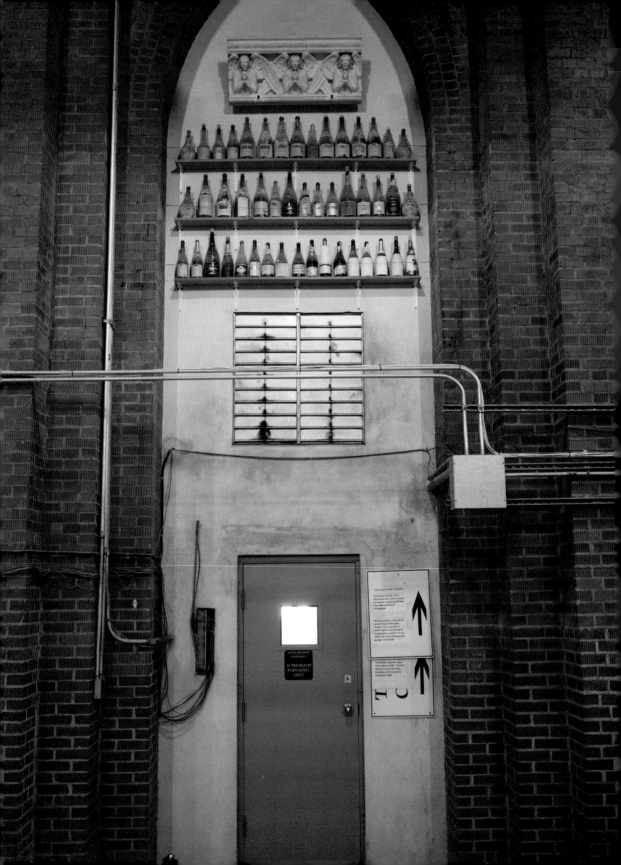

WASHINGTON NATIONAL CATHEDRAL

A Braille plaque worn from touch is the only public indication that the Washington National Cathedral serves as the final resting place for activist Helen Keller. Keller and her lifelong companion and teacher, Anne Sullivan Macy, are interred in the crypt below the massive cathedral, an area strictly off limits to the general public. It's one of many unexpected aspects of the neo-Gothic landmark.

"This place always surprises me," says the cathedral's chief communication officer, Kevin Eckstrom, as he points out some of the lesser-seen highlights and views of the building that was started in 1907 but was not completed until eighty-three years later in 1990. "You never stop learning about this building or its history."

A peek at what Eckstrom refers to as the "attic" reveals a long, narrow space where a little bit of everything shows up, including outdated AV equipment, a suit of armor, and an old card catalogue filled with handwritten donation cards from fund-raising campaigns gone by. "Here's one from a donor in 1973 who gave us twenty-five dollars," he says, holding a card from one of the long drawers. "There even are some in here from people who sent us fifty cents."

Not far from the attic, near the base of a spiral staircase leading up to the top of the central tower, rows of dusty champagne bottles line narrow shelves placed above a staff door. Beginning around 1960, the stonemasons would raise a glass to the new year every December. Cathedral lore has it that the tradition began when some stone carvers felt

snubbed by the official office party, so they held their own in this spot. The old bottles represent about thirty years of gatherings.

"My name is on some of those," says Jay Carpenter, who worked at the cathedral for twenty years as a stone carver. "Sometimes it was very low key, and sometimes a lot of guests would come in and it would be more of an event. Much has been made of it."

A few weeks before the 2011 DC-area earthquake that damaged the cathedral, one of the carvers coincidentally reinforced the makeshift installation with guy wire, undoubtedly keeping the bottles from smashing to the ground during the 5.8 quake.

The handiwork of the carvers can be seen throughout the structure, which officially is named the Cathedral Church of Saint Peter and Saint Paul in the City and Diocese of Washington. It also can be seen on the structure through the many gargoyles, angels, and grotesques that embellish the towers. "Gargoyles have water spouts in their mouths while grotesques do not," Eckstrom points out. "A gargoyle is a grotesque with a pipe in its mouth."

Star Wars fans often use binoculars—along with the force and instructions provided by the cathedral—to spy the Darth Vader grotesque up on the northwest tower. Sculpted by Carpenter, the fallen Jedi figure came about as the result of a design-your-own-carving contest for kids held in the 1980s. Vader came in third, but his legacy lives on, while the other two depict now mostly forgotten pop culture fads.

The carvers got personal with some of the angels atop the central tower. "A lot of the images you see here are based on people who worked on them," says Eckstrom. Others share moments of institutional pride, like the one holding an Academy Award. The angel's face is that of Marjorie Hunt, who directed and produced a short documentary about the cathedral stone carvers. She took home an Oscar for the film in 1985. Still at work on the building, the artists decided to commemorate her win in stone.

Other noteworthy occasions are less permanently but still majestically marked at

the Washington National Cathedral by the ringing of bells. The cathedral is the only church in America that can claim both a ten-bell peal and a carillon in a single tower. A steel cable connects each of the carillon bells to what looks like a keyboard, allowing the carillonneur to play the heavy bells, some of which weigh several tons, through what acts like a piano console. Members of the Washington Ringer Society and a select group of students from the Whitechapel Guild of the National Cathedral School for Girls play the peal bells by pulling on long ropes. Unlike the carillon, the peal bells play mathematical patterns rather than melodies.

It's possible to open the windows in the circular bell room and walk out onto a stone catwalk. Getting out the window takes a bit of a leap, while sidestepping the cliché of referring to the panoramic view of the city as heavenly is the tougher maneuver up here. "This is the only place in the city where you can look down at the Washington Monument," says Eckstrom. "This is the highest point in the city. The Washington Monument is taller than we are, but we are up higher."

WESCHLER'S AUCTION HOUSE

John Wilkes Booth escaped on horseback across this alley on that fateful 1865 night. A hundred and fifty-two years later, a steady stream of highest bidders backs up through it to haul away the newly found treasures they won at Weschler's final auction within DC city limits.

Housed in a five-story building at 905 E Street, NW, the family-run business has been auctioning off items since 1890. Today, even as they run the last sale, the current generation of Weschlers is packing up for brand-new digs in Rockville. Partly filled boxes occupy every corner of the deep building that has been Weschler's Auctioneers & Appraisers since 1945. Prior to that, it operated nearby on Pennsylvania Avenue.

Just as they have for years, the weekly public auctions bring out serious shoppers and regular spectators who nibble cookies from the free tray put out on a scratched end table. Some eat their brown bag lunches or do the crossword puzzles while waiting for the action to begin. Would-be buyers circle the lots of second-hand merchandise, examining the piles upon piles of goods marked with numbers that will be used to iden tify them. Pretty much anything that has or can be found in an attic, gallery, or estate sale shows up at the Tuesday first-floor sale, from garden sculptures to floral china services for forty, to a beige La-Z-Boy recliner that winds up going for a dollar. Higher-end items get sold from the second floor, with its more formal auction setup.

Above the auction floors are offices, a fine arts cage, and thousands of square feet of stuff. A photo backdrop used to capture items for catalogues remains partially set

up near a window with three sections united by a rounded semicircle up top. Light from E Street filters through it. The arc creates a contrast of shapes with the large section of uniform square windows it frames from the building across the street, which happens to be the backside of FBI headquarters.

"This is my favorite spot in the building," says Client Services and Administrative Manager Karen Weschler, who used to come down to this office with her dad as a kid to help the unending stream of boxes that came in for auction. "I love that window."

But this business doesn't leave much time for sentimentality. Downstairs the sale begins. Her brother and cousin begin announcing the lots, the distinct auctioneer's tempo setting the pace.

"It is bittersweet," she remarks, and glances toward the window. Then it's back to work.

WOLF TRAP NATIONAL PARK FOR THE PERFORMING ARTS

Taking in a show while stretched out on a blanket on the lawn at Wolf Trap stands as a sacred summertime ritual for many a Washingtonian. Veterans from summers past strategize on how to win the lawn dash to their preferred picnic spots once the gates open and often carry their favorite vintage while completing the sprint. They also tend to have strong opinions on where to grab a spot in the parking lot to avoid postconcert traffic jams. What even seasoned Wolf Trap loyalists do not typically have is an eye on the world backstage at the only national park for the performing arts.

On the lesser-seen side of the stage, the inner workings of the wings of the outdoor amphitheater, like the extensive pulley system, create a dramatic effect before anyone ever steps on stage. "It's so beautiful that it's almost a work of art," says Michelle Pendoley, former director of public relations for Wolf Trap.

Named for Catherine Filene Shouse, who donated the land and the money for the outdoor theater, the Filene Center's vast backstage exudes a practical beauty. For those who headline here, it starts when tour buses pull up to the back of the theater. Unlike other concert venues, the loading docks are framed by the Douglas fir and southern yellow pine planks of the performance structure. The green of the

park contrasts with the brown of the wood, generating a backdrop for the backdrop. For the few who get to look out from the center stage at a full house and the lawn beyond it, they truly are seeing the full vision the architects and founders had for this place, Pendoley says.

Occasionally, musicians who grace the Filene Center's stage leave behind more than a song as crooner Tony Bennett did after a show. Hanging in the Wolf Trap offices, a small watercolor the singer painted of the site is another incarnation of the works of art that can be found beyond the spotlights of Wolf Trap.

ZERO MILESTONE

All roads lead here. At least that was the plan.

About one hundred years ago, this spot on the Ellipse was chosen as the country's zero mile marker, the place from where all roads would be measured. In 1919, the government set down a temporary marker, with the official one following in 1923. Much fanfare surrounded its placement with comparisons to the Golden Milestone of Ancient Rome flowing like spiced wine.

"My countrymen, in the old Roman forum there was erected in the days of Rome's greatness a golden milestone," President Warren G. Harding said during the 1923 Zero Milestone dedication ceremony. "From it was measured and marked the system of highways which gridironed the Roman world and bound the uttermost provinces to the heart and center of the empire. We are dedicating here another golden milestone, to which we and those after us will relate the wide-ranging units of the highway system of this country."

Spoiler alert: It never happened.

Nowadays the main function of the four-foot-high granite marker topped with a bronze compass rose is to serve as a place for sightseers to set down their water bottles while they snap photos of the White House. Its height also seems to speak to weary travelers in need of a place to lean before conquering the rest of the city.

ACKNOWLEDGMENTS

No Access Washington, DC, is a book because a wonderful group of people helped us to take it from idea to the page. These people not only trusted us enough to allow us to visit places precious to them, to the city, and to history, but welcomed us warmly. In many cases that meant allowing us into sites not typically open to the general public sites, which we understand can be a big ask. So many people along the way were generous with their time and their stories, and for that we are so appreciative. Thank you to the following individuals for allowing us into your worlds, for supporting this project, suggesting places, brainstorming, making introductions, issuing permits, visiting sites with us, answering questions, sharing information, showing us around, and so much more:

Alex Dodds, Alli Weiss, Anthony Hesselius, Ari Geller, Audrey Fix Schaefer, Audrey Tepper, Austin Graff, Betsy Gressler, Brian Joyner, Carol McDonald, Chana Engle, Craig Fifer, Debra Perlin, Denise at Road Runner Photography, Elizabeth Buchanan, Elizabeth Baudhuin, Emily Levine, Gay Vietzke, Grace Tumminelli, Gretchen Ellsworth, Hanaa Rifaey, Helen von Gohren, Jackie Leventhal, Jim McKinney, John Shore, Juan Moreno, Karen Weschler, Kate Childs Graham, Kerry Wilson, Kristen Gentile, Shannon Powers, Lindley Thornburg Richardson, Lisa Grant, Marvin Mostow, Matt Weiss, Meagan Baco, Mel Gold, Michelle Weiner, Miriam Kleiman, Mioko Miller, Mistue Morita, Nicholas Partridge, Rachel Zukrow, Rebecca Goodstein, Robbin Owen, Sara Adland, Sara Jaffe, Sarah Rosenfeld, Sean Kennealy, Sioux Thompson, Spencer Abruzzese, Susan McCullough, Tara Morrison, Tom Jacobus, Tonya Thomas, Tina O'Connell, and Tom Fazzini.

A tremendous thank-you to Eric Parnes for allowing us to include his striking images of the former Iranian embassy on pages 38–39 and for sharing his experience.

A special thank-you to Steve Coleman of Washington Parks & People for your generosity of time, spirit, and hope, and for sharing your parks and lore with us.

Amy Lyons, I cannot thank you enough for entrusting me with this project. I feel lucky to have the opportunity to work with you once more and to have the chance to write about Washington, DC, again. Thank you to Hope Clarke and the editorial and publicity and marketing teams at Globe Pequot Press for your care and attention.

Emily, it's been another wonderful adventure. Thank you for your eye and your images—and for being good company along the way.

I am incredibly lucky in my life to have a group of people who support and lift me up in life and through the process of *No Access Washington, DC.* For your support and friendship as well as your check-ins, pep talks, skillful edits, field trip companionship, introductions, and understanding of this deadline, thank you: Alyson Weinberg, Courtney Farber, Debbie Feit, Sharon Samber, Lisa Kanter, Jonathan Kanter, Jessica Nemeth, Ilana Preuss, Louise Milkman, and Mark Katkov.

I cannot let the chance go by without acknowledging that the spirit and life of Elissa Froman dances throughout these pages. She showed up at just about every site visit in this book, and for that I am grateful.

To my extraordinary DC-born and -bred children, Miriam and Gabriel, who help me smile on and off deadline. I like and love you both more than there are words to say.

Jeff, who knew all those years ago that DC would be the place? That it would be home? Thanks for being you.

—BKK

Turns out, getting access to the hidden and off-limits spots in and around DC requires lots of special permission. And by special permission, I mean folks who know us, vouching that we'd be good stewards of sacred, historic, precious places and convincing many layers of gatekeepers that we could be trusted with access that very few others get.

As such, this book is the product of a huge community of wildly helpful people:

Alex Dodds, Alli Weiss, Anthony Hesselius, Ari Geller, Betsy Gressler, Carol McDonald, Chana Engle, Courtney Farber, Craig Fifer, Debra Perlin, Devin Dotson, Elizabeth Buchanan, Emily Levine, Hanaa Rifaey, Jackie Leventhal, John Shore, Kate Childs Graham, Kristen Gentile, Lisa Dubler, Marvin Mostow, Michelle Weiner, Rachel Zukrow, Ryan Thomas, Sara Adland, Sara Jaffe, Sioux Thompson, Spencer Abruzzese, Susan McCullough, and Tom Fazzini.

Thank you for connecting us and trusting us.

To Beth Kanter, your ability to dream, ask, visualize, then create is stunning. Thanks for inviting me along on this adventure! And to Amy Lyons at Rowman & Littlefield, thank you for once again believing I was the right gal to photograph this project.

Knowing that Steve Coleman at Washington Parks & People is doing such awe-inspiring work on a daily basis gives me hope for our city and our world.

Amy Born, Cara Fisher, Amber Wobschall, Ori Korin, Jodi Holzband, and Molly Amster—you are my rocks. Thank you for checking in, brainstorming, and liking so many of my posts on social media.

To my parents, Lois and Peter Goodstein, thank you for choosing DC and teaching me to love it, too.

To my sister Rebecca Goodstein, I wish I could have brought you with me on every single location we visited for this book! Your love of our city and powerful work to be a good steward of the environment makes me so proud to be your sister.

To my sister Sarah Rosenfeld, I cried in the lobby of the NIH Clinical Center during our photo session as I told the staff your heroic story. Your bravery is inspiring.

And lastly, to my very patient partner, Ron Kelly: Thank you for listening and encouraging me. And teaching me to appreciate a well-designed parking lot. Life would be far less exciting, less delicious, and significantly less interesting without you in it.

—EPG

ABOUT
BETH KANTER

Beth has written a number of books about her favorite city including *Day Trips from Washington, DC; Washington, DC Chef's Table; Food Lovers' Guide to Washington, DC;* and *Great Food Finds Washington, DC.* Her essays and articles have appeared in national newspapers, magazines, and online. Beth has an MSJ from Northwestern's Medill School of Journalism and teaches writing workshops. Join her on Instagram at @beekaekae.

ABOUT
EMILY PEARL
GOODSTEIN

Emily is a digital strategy consultant, sheet cake enthusiast, photographer, and rabble rouser from Washington, DC. She loves oversharing on social media—follow along at @emilygoodstein for restaurant suggestions and other insider info.